I Wept by the Rivers of Babylon

A prisoner of conscience in a time of war

Terry Edwin Walstrom

Conscience

I believe the foundation of conscience begins and ends with the unwillingness to harm others or to allow harm by inaction. As the Talmud teaches:

Whoever saves one life saves the world entire.

I WEPT BY THE RIVERS OF BABYLON:

A PRISONER OF CONSCIENCE
IN A TIME OF WAR

TERRY EDWIN WALSTROM

COPYRIGHT © 2013 by Terry Walstrom

All rights reserved. No part of this work may be reproduced or transmitted in any form by any means, electronic or mechanical including photocopying and recording or by any information storage or retrieval system without permission in writing from the author.

By the rivers of Babylon we sat and wept

We sang songs for our tormentors...

ACKNOWLEDGEMENTS

I very much wish to thank the following persons:
Doug Mason, for format and clarity.
marvinshilmer.blogspot.com
Front & back cover design: Ruud Rozemeijer
Quentin Roberts, loyal friend.
Editors: Patsy Paschal, Bob Titiryn.
My beloved children:
Laura, Jason, Vanessa, Terry, Nicholas, Lillian and Helena.
Friend Dub Horn, who showed me what alternate service really means.
James Hill, who knows it all without being a *know-it-all*.

(Cover drawing by T.E. Walstrom ©1965)

DEDICATION

I dedicate this book to my Brothers in bondage 1967-1969 in Seagoville Federal Correctional Institution.

We did the best we could to be men of integrity.

The warmth of our fellowship I carry in my heart to the end of my days.

So many of us have gone forever.

Goodbye Sam and Danny; I hope you have found peace.

Table of Contents

Introduction i
Certainty and the Absolute iii
Rituals of Certainty viii
Clash of Certainties ix
I Wept By The Rivers Of Babylon Part I:
My Personal Journey As A Conscientious Objector 1
(1952) Child God 3
(1953) Sunday school 3
1958-1963 Horror 12
   Draft Classifications during the Vietnam War 29
August 1966 33
   Historical note: Cassius Clay 35
1966 Draft Board 37
Court-Appointed Attorney 49
Conversations with Myself 55
Sunk-Cost Fallacy 61
1967 Lesson Number One 62
Rack Time 69
Transfer 71
Seagoville 72
1967-1969 Seagoville Nemesis 82
The Belly of the Beast 84
Later 89
Capacity for Violence 93

Aftermath 94
Final Argument to the Jury 94
Hospital Service 98
Old Friends, no Amends 111

**I Wept By The Rivers Of Babylon Part II:
Tracing The History Of Conscience** 115
Legacy of Constantine 116
Early Church Fathers 117
Change of Attitude 119
Paradigm Shift 120
What is the Just War? 122
Conscience Arises 123
Modern Pacifism 125
Contrary Argument 125
Conscription Meets Conscience 128
Vietnam War 1959-1975 133
Denominations Grapple with War 135
    Mormons 136
    Catholics 136
    Protestants 137
    Hutterites 138
    Seventh-day Adventists 139
Medal of Honor for a Conscientious Objector 144
Conclusions 151
Confounding God and Caesar 152
Joseph Franklin Rutherford 154

"Worse than traitors" 161
   Letters to Bible Students in Military Camps.............. 164
Aftermath 165
Jehovah's Witnesses vs. Superior Authorities 166
   First Amendment actions before the Supreme Court
   166
Nazi Era... 171
Chutzpah... 178
Biased Neutrality 180
Trouble in America 182
Promise of Absolute Certainty 186
Irony... 187
The Rest of the Story 188
Bibliography 197

INTRODUCTION

The Purple Heart is a badge of military merit awarded to men wounded or killed in the line of duty for extraordinary bravery and valor. Many are awarded posthumously.

When I was a young boy sitting on my grandmother's lap she read to me from a book about WWII.

A section listing the names of soldiers awarded Purple Hearts included the description of their heroic actions.

Page after page described men who threw their own bodies over a live hand grenade to protect their Fellow soldiers in a foxhole!

My child's mind could not grasp such an action. I asked, "Why?"

"Greater love hath no man," my grandmother whispered to me, *"than he lay down his life for his friend."*

The first Christian martyr, Stephen, was stoned to death for blasphemy, we are told in Holy Scripture. The Catholic Church regards him as Saint Stephen yet, what Christian ever asks: Why was a blasphemer made a Saint!?

The scripture reveals authorities in the synagogue listened to Stephen's testimony then, voted by stoning him to death.

From the perspective of a Christian, Stephen is venerated as the model of righteous faith.

From the viewpoint of devout Jewish purists of the 1st century: apostate enemy. What are we to conclude?

One man's apostate is another man's hero and saint.

Evil men hijacked airliners filled with innocent passengers and flew them into the World Trade Center. Why did terrorists believe with an absolute certainty their promised reward was more precious than human lives?

Q: Are all martyrs equal? A: It comes down to this:

Just because you are absolutely certain you have God, science or public opinion on your side—there is no guarantee you won't end up committing the deeds of a monster! The bottom line is, once again, are you willing to see others harmed in order to achieve your goals?

The conscientious objector comes face to face with very determined authorities who themselves are absolutely certain. We all need to take a step back and examine exactly what that state of mind can lead to.

CERTAINTY AND THE ABSOLUTE

In the Physics Department the Professor gathers his students on the first day of class to a gymnasium for a demonstration. The class is intrigued, curious and eager to observe.

The Professor begins...

"In science there are things we are certain of to the point we call them *laws.* They are true invariably because we test them and the results are always the same. Scientists depend on them and you should too. Some things we are sure of but we are guessing. Other things we might bet money on but we all know that is called gambling. Let's get to the nitty-gritty of the greatest challenge to the human intellect.

Shall we demonstrate the full implications of absolute certainty?" The Professor grins and walks over to the suspended wrecking ball hanging from a cable in the ceiling of the gym.

"Isaac Newton discovered: For every action there is an *equal* and *opposite* reaction. This is called a Law of Motion."

The Professor gazes around at the students, appraising awareness.

"There is also a Law of Conservation of Energy. What it means is you never get more out of a system than you put into it. In other words, in the entire Universe there is no free ride!"

Then with a sly smile he concludes: "Who believes what I said is true?"

All hands go up easily. The Professor flashes his wicked smile.

"Remember, I said this is a Law of Science. How many of you are absolutely certain?" Nobody hesitates; all hands remain up.

"Very well, let me test your convictions. I need a volunteer."

An athletic looking "jock" student ambles forward with a swagger.

"I'm your Huckleberry." The other students giggle.

"Thank you, *Huck*. I'm going to have you step 10 feet back and away from the ball."

The student counts off as he steps careful paces backward.

"As you all observe, I am holding on to this one hundred pound wrecking ball. I'm facing our brave volunteer, old Huck, over there." (He gives a little wave.)

"Wonder what I am going to do next? I'm now slowly pushing and walking it forward until …"

The cable holding the ball stretches tight. The Professor labors to hold the ball in place; arms stretch forward like a cop stopping traffic, one half inch from the volunteer's nose…

"I am going to release this iron ball and it is going to swing away from your tender exposed face. The action of gravity will, upon release, cause an opposite reaction. It will send it all the way to the other side. Energy is still a part of the momentum so it will, after a pause, rush back again toward the starting point: your face. Oh yes, back toward your face!"

He looks directly at the volunteer.

The jock shakes his head like he's just heard really unbelievably bad news. The students grow loud and agitated.

"Rejoice, because there is friction in the system and gravity is exerting a counter force deducting energy from the system. The Law says energy will be *conserved* and this ball will not and cannot reach your nose."

"Since you believe the Law of Conservation of Energy will not allow this ball to come any closer than it is now, you cannot possibly have your head smashed to a bloody pulp by impact. That would mean more energy somehow magically inserted itself into the system which science tells us is *hardly* possible."

Immediately the volunteer vanishes back into the crowd to the roar of unmerciful booing and catcalls! The Professor nods knowingly.

"Anybody else want to show their absolute certainty?" Several candidates are unwillingly offered by the crowd but each one shakes loose and declines in protest.

"Very well, then. I, myself, shall demonstrate confidence and my own absolute certainty. When you test your belief it is either confirmed or disconfirmed."

The Professor, with the help of two others, stands where the volunteer had stood. He closes his eyes and screws up his face in anticipation of the worst.

He signals and the helpers push the ball up to his nose and let go.

Immediately, the ball swings directly away from him in a ponderously slow arc across the gym and pauses 20 feet away. With the sure swiftness of a freight train it hurls ominously forward on a dead ahead path toward the Professor's fragile skull! At the last possible millisecond the ball pauses at maximum arc a little more than an inch from his outstretched nose and return swings ever backward again! (A collective *gasp* issues from the witnesses at the instant of near contact.)

Dead silence, then groans, screams and a cheer burst out as the demonstration comes to a dramatic conclusion. Thunderous applause erupts as the students hail the bravado of the Professor and laugh in relief.

"What are you cheering and why? This was not 'faith' on my part. Science isn't true because smart people SAY it is true. It is true because anybody can perform these experiments for themselves. Anybody, anywhere in the world at any time achieves the identical response.

"Science is about testing, experimenting and trying to disprove your own ideas. What is true does not belong to an elite governing body of elders. It belongs to everybody everywhere.

"This is why science works and we have technology and medicine instead of witch doctors and priests in hospitals, at NASA and in University. Okay?

"Now, go and do likewise. Class dismissed."

*****

Question: What is the difference between superstition, religion and science in terms of certainty of outcome?

Do rituals serve the same function in religion as they do in science?

Rituals of Certainty

In a primitive society dancing "brings" rain. How? The dance is continued until the rain falls! Hours, days, weeks pass by until rain comes. Ritual persistence seemingly trumps reality, or *so it appears.* Failure is to the true believer a spur to invest even greater persistence in the ritual behavior! The rain dance continues as long as it must. To stop short of the desired result is an act of *apostasy* to the (false) premise. Rituals confirm loyalty to belief itself.

CLASH OF CERTAINTIES

In 1616, the Catholic Church was absolutely certain these words of the Holy Bible were true: "the world is firmly established and it cannot be moved." Galileo, an astronomer, offered a contradictory view: the world turns! The Holy Office issued a condemnation of Galileo's theory declaring the idea, the Sun stood still and the Earth moved, was false and he was forbidden to hold the idea in his mind or defend it. He was called to appear before Inquisitors.

The custom of the legal system in Europe at that time under Catholic authority was to display instruments of torture while any questioning was being conducted. After weighing the pros and cons of scientific certainty vs. dead certainty of torture, Galileo *recanted* and was placed under house arrest for the remainder of his life.

Even so, the Catholic Church today acknowledges Galileo's condemnation was wrong. The astronomer died in 1642. The Church apologized in 1992. Did God correct them? The Vatican issued two stamps of Galileo as an expression of regret for his mistreatment.[1]

The clash between science and Church authority was a clash of certainties.

The astronomer tested his certainty against reality and became convinced of the truth of the movement of the Earth. The Church declared his telescope provided evidence of Satan and refused to open faith to the possibility of disconfirmation. The Age of Reason hit them like a wrecking ball.

There is an apocryphal version of this story which ends with Galileo whispering: "Yet, it moves." We might ask *who* reported that version.

Does the Catholic Church deserve kudos for eventually changing the official opinion in the face of hundreds of years of scientific encroachment into their domain?

Did God correct them or was the preponderance of evidence so embarrassing as to force their hand?

Authority vested by claim to God's approval and guidance might logically welcome any tests from any quarter which would serve to bolster and affirm the truth of those claims.

Could it equally be said unwillingness to hear arguments testing claims of authority is an *admission*?

---

[1] http://www.catholic.com/tracts/the-galileo-controversy
Bernadeane Carr, STL, Censor Librorum August 10, 2004

I Wept By The Rivers Of Babylon
Part I:

My Personal Journey As A Conscientious Objector

— MY STORY—

Nobody can tell you the story the way it really happened. I'm going to tell it the way I remember it.

"The ultimate measure of a man is not where he stands in moments of convenience, but where he stands in moments of challenge, moments of great crisis and controversy."
— Martin Luther King Jr. —

"All you have to do is write one true sentence. Write the truest sentence that you know."
— Ernest Hemingway—

"It's always difficult to keep personal prejudice out of a thing like this. And wherever you run into it, prejudice always obscures the truth. I don't really know what the truth is. I don't suppose anybody will ever really know. Nine of us now seem to feel the defendant is innocent, but we're just gambling on probabilities - we may be wrong. We may be trying to let a guilty man go free, I don't know. Nobody really can. But we have a reasonable doubt and that's something that's very valuable in our system. No jury can declare a man guilty unless it's sure."
— Juror #8, Twelve Angry Men—

"Every man dies, but not every man really lives."
— William Wallace—

(1952) CHILD GOD

As a child, God was for me like the sunrise at morning. God was as real as the moon. Sometimes God was the darkness of midnight, as warm as the summer heat inside my lonely room.

Yet, never had I been to a church or cathedral and I knew nothing of verses of scripture and candles or spires.

I was an *innocent*, drunk on the passions of childhood's persuasion—soon to expire.

(1953) SUNDAY SCHOOL

In my own front yard, hanging from the limb of my favorite tree, listening to a hundred cicadas scraping away in the hot summer sunshine, a rumbling came.

A large yellow bus rolled under the shade trees and squeaked to a stop. A burly stranger emerged. He stalked straight over to my tree as though he meant to startle me. He surely did!

I had been cautioned: never talk to strangers!

His bright yellow bus wobbled with cantankerous children whose clamors now reached me clear across the grassy patch of yard. Black letters stenciled along the vehicle's side read:

VACATION BIBLE SCHOOL

I slipped off the tree branch and landed like a spooked cat on my feet as the large man approached and spoke.

"Which church do *you* attend, son?"

It was unthinkable that I not answer.

"None!" I blurted.

I wasn't sure why a sense of shame crept over me. I had a vague notion everybody probably ought to go to church. Maybe I'd heard kids at school talk about which church *they* attended. Yet, shame it was.

The bus driver blotted out the sun. I was standing in his shadow as he spoke in a low, gentle voice.

"Your parents don't make you go to Sunday school?"

There was wonderment in his tone. I felt heat welling up in my cheeks.

"I don't have a Dad. My parents divorced." I whispered.

My entire world in one soft sentence! W*hy* had I said it?

In my sullen imagination I was *inferior* and defective.

A boy without a Father may be a bastard!

I was confessing the last thing I wanted any soul to know, suspect or think.

The bus man studied me as a kid looks at spiders with a magnifying glass and an attitude of cringing wonder.

"I need to talk to your Mom. Do you live in this house?" His voice left no room for anything but truth.

"I live here, uh huh."

I pointed at the duplex on concrete blocks behind him.

The dark rectangle of a man loped over to the first door at the top of three steps.

Before he could knock, I could see my grandma positioned behind the other screen door. She spoke.

I really didn't want to hear anything they said to each other. If I didn't move or listen or think about what was being said it might magically render me invisible. It would be like hiding under the covers from a monster.

The adult conversation was brief. *I hadn't moved even half an inch.*

"I spoke to your grandma and told her all children need to be at their Creator's house on Sabbath. So, I'll be picking you up next Sunday in that bus over there at 9 am sharp; unless I'm early or late. Be clean. Be ready."

No smile.

He gave me a look which seemed to say, 'Do you understand English?'

I just shrugged and nodded.

"I'm Brother Branch." He continued staring at me expecting something. I determined to hold my breath and slip from notice.

"And, what is your name?" He finally asked with quiet exasperation.

"Oh, um-Terry."

He cocked his head a bit allowing my words to slide into memory, nodded, turned and left.

As abruptly as the incident began he was back on the bus. A rude sound ground away at the gears until every part of the yellow mirage vanished in a shimmering puff of dust and smoky sunlight.

Immediately I let out a lung full of pent up air in a slow *whoosh*, trembling as though a big dog had wandered onto the property and opted not to bite me.

I felt a little relief.

I was surrounded by a copse of rustling green branches overhead whispering warnings in the wind.

Something still bothered me. A sense of dread welled up.

I was obligated to God. I was *obligated* to God…

One week to the day, there I stood on my front porch scanning the highway. A five-year-old-boy all slicked up in an uncomfortable white shirt and slacks; I waited. Inside my pocket was a rolled up dollar bill my Maw-maw offered, which she explained was for contribution or collection sure to come.

Inside my head felt like a hive of angry bees.

All I knew is I was obligated. No escape. God was coming for me in a rickety yellow bus.

Sundays were good for swinging on a long rope and yodeling my Tarzan yell. Not today.

I had no notion of what to expect or what was expected *of* me.

Bashful around strangers and without charm or guile, I was the very portrait of a pathetic child who, it seems, somehow begs to be teased.

Photographs of me until the age of eighteen portray a hang dog countenance.

Adults greeted me for the first time with "What's wrong; are you okay?"

Vibrations in the air preceded the torture of gears and the manhandled yellow vehicle coughed into view. I trudged forward as a prisoner to the gallows.

The mouth of the beast opened and swallowed me whole.

The bus ride to Brother Branch's church was merriment for teasers and bullies. My share of the fun was as you might expect. I was taunted for having a "girl's name."

The little morons of the Sunday School bully squad were good little Christians one and all.

Suffer the children.

I grasped the passenger strap as close to the bus driver as I could manage.

Brother Branch completely ignored all screaming and horseplay as no adult I'd ever witnessed! One bellow from his barrel chest surely would have quelled the riot and sent the flock scattering as lambs fleeing a bolt of lightning.

No such luck. Brother Branch drove furiously across every terrain as though testing the aptitude of guardian angels.

All passengers disgorged and shepherded into a crowded Sunday school classroom upon arrival. The interior room revealed itself ordinary and secular in every way…

Except for one jarring detail…

Walls stood littered with dozens of badly colored Bible characters tacked everywhere. Helter-skelter assaulted my wondering eyes!

Religious-themed coloring books passed around our table with boxes of ill-treated crayons heaped into a community pile.

This bounty was swiftly set upon by filthy hands and nimble fingers. Purple and green Bible heroes from tiny, feverish, hallucinating Christian minds were fashioned.

Floating halos suggested Jesus' head was the object of a celestial ring toss!

I recalled the shortest verse of scripture in Maw-maw's Catholic Bible:

"Jesus wept."

My own drawing of Daniel in the den of lions wore sympathetic expression of confident woe.

Our kindly lady of the blue hair and twinkly glasses informed us our talent was *miraculous*. Then, like wretched swine, she herded us squealing into the main Church auditorium for adult services!

Blood of the lamb

My first interior glimpse of stained glass and candles, *numinous* artifacts and solemn faces in service to Almighty God! I sniffed the acrid mixture of old lady perfume, cheap after shave and little boy sweat. Bedazzling pearl necklaces, beehive hairdos and glowing cheek rouge swarmed like portraits in a fevered dream of manikins.

Impressions were clear and direct: these people were *unhinged.* Why spend a perfectly good Sunday posed in uncomfortable clothing standing and sitting and standing again? Was God hard up for entertainment? Why would God need this or think of it in the first place?

An adult beside me offered to share her Hymnal. I was not familiar with such a masculine word!

Opening the gilded book, a row of serious and stilted verses proclaimed an endless caterwaul of Praises.

Organ music made me mindful of Grandma's radio soap operas. Pepper Young's Family, Search for Tomorrow, The Guiding Light.

These were sponsored by Ajax, the foaming cleanser. (Wash the dirt right down the drain.) I could sing *that.*

The collection plate passed like a bucket brigade at a fire. I tugged the sweaty dollar bill from my pocket to quench the flames of hell. All the while, up at the lectern, a voluminous voice volleyed praises admonishing goodness and forbearance from sin.

Thoughts dulled and somehow I drifted until I beheld the entire congregation rapt in intense scrutiny of the floor itself! No. It was a moment of prayer!

"Why look *down* when speaking to God who is surely *up*?" I wondered.

Church folk screwed their eyes intensely shut. Some gripped the Bible in their wrinkled hands as a thrumming energy caught the air.

What was coming?

The mood changed ominously. Spindly arms waved about, then, a swaying of bodies, gibbering voices: calling, answering, rattling. Soon, lowing noises erupted as shivering folk dropped to the floor.

"Booth led boldly with his big bass drum—
(Are you washed in the blood of the Lamb?)
The Saints smiled gravely and they said: "He's come."
(Are you washed in the blood of the Lamb?)
Walking lepers followed, rank on rank,
Lurching bravos from the ditches dank,
Drabs from the alleyways and drug fiends pale—
Minds still passion-ridden, soul-powers frail.—
Vermin-eaten saints with moldy breath,
Unwashed legions with the ways of Death—
(Are you washed in the blood of the Lamb?)"[2]

My head was pounding! A dizzy fear suddenly engulfed my soul.

A strong hand *pulled* at me.

The next moment I found myself alone in a small, cramped cloak room. Someone entered. Brother Branch was removing his cassock, shirt and *trousers*. All the while, his voice thrummed and wavered as the organ swelled. The congregation moaned.

Now, the echoes!

---

[2] *General William Booth Enters Into Heaven*, music by Charles Ives, lyric by Vachel Lindsay

Are you washed?

                Are you washed?

Are you washed?

                Are you washed?
                IN THE BLOOD?

On the bus ride back to my house I continued shaking. What in the world was *that* all about? I knew one thing for certain; I would not return to Church! The Sabbath was a kind of vile Halloween. I solemnly understood those three words: Fear-of-God.

God roared off spitting gravel and smoke while I stood stunned at my own curbside. The neighborhood did not look the same.

Inside my house, Maw-maw softly inquired of the day's experience.

I shuffled a bit and squirmed as though my skin were clothed in nettles. If I lied and said it was okay, surely the whole ordeal would be revisited upon me.

If I said I hated it, I would offend God.

"I'd much rather spend the day with you, Maw-maw!"

Her face flickered with surprised pleasure.

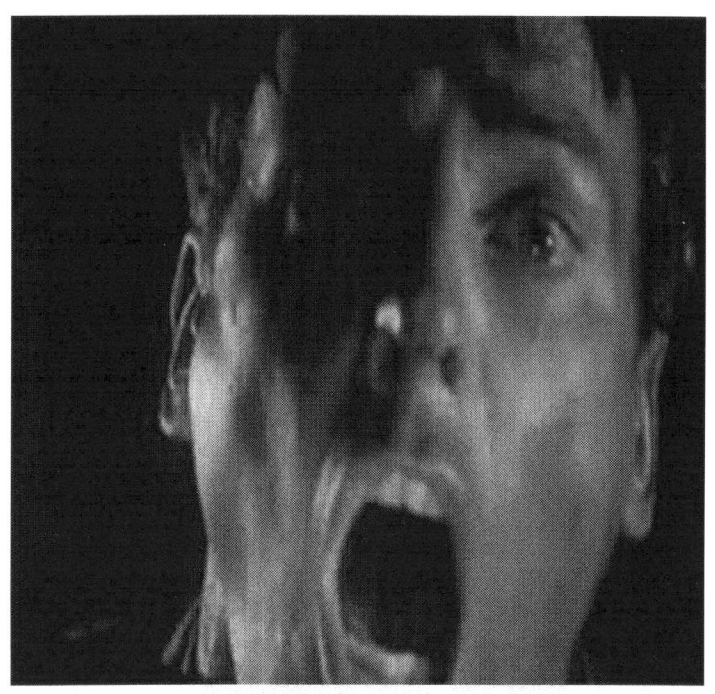

1958-1963 HORROR

William Castle's Fan Club was an idea doomed from the beginning. Castle directed cheap horror films with gimmicks such as The Tingler, (hidden buzzers activated under your theatre seat); Macabre (movie patrons were insured for one million dollars against death by fright). You might say the allure was better than the films. I was just a kid though, what did I care? I had acquired a taste for all things science-fiction, horror and dinosaurs.

The Worth, in Downtown Fort Worth, was a lavish Egyptian-style vaudeville palace converted into a movie theater. I arrived with my younger cousin, Debbie, and we found the room upstairs where the Fan Club was scheduled to meet.

We both hoped we might meet other fans or get discount tickets.

One kid with glasses, named Johnny, with freckles, clothes a size too small and a tight-lipped expression, appeared in charge. He was my age. We kicked around a few notions but it was going nowhere. Nothing came of the idea or the Fan Club. Well, not exactly *nothing*…

Months later Johnny recognized me on my way home from school. We renewed acquaintance. In fact, we took to each other for probably no greater reason than our mutual love of monsters, horror and science fiction! Ours was an alternate universe and my first real friendship. It was for me, momentous!

I learned Johnny was a JW (Jehovah's Witness) as well as a big horror movie buff. I had no clue how *that* worked. Religion was not for me. On the other hand, famous monsters of film land were something of much greater interest. Oh, but it didn't take long for his religion to cast a few shadows on the friendship.

Once he started talking there was no end of the subject. I sometimes wondered which meant the most to Johnny: Jehovah or the Creature from the Black Lagoon. It was all the same to me. After chattering about movies, girls, bike rides, music and other interests, the topic turned toward God. My buddy never missed an opportunity to swing conversation around to a religious lesson, observation or query.

Johnny would ask peculiar questions I was supposed to answer on the spot!

"Did you know Jesus didn't have a beard?"

He may as well have asked if I knew that a bear didn't poop in the woods. How do you reply to something as crazy as that?

"I give up—why didn't Jesus have a beard?" I half expected a punch line to a joke.

But, no, I was informed about paintings in the catacombs and a chalice with a clean-cut Jesus and blah blah-blah. Everybody has some weird thing they believe, so, no big deal.

I think I was supposed to admire Johnny's grasp of these enchanting tidbits.

"Did you know there is no burning hell?"

"Did you know we don't have a soul—we *are* a soul?"

"Did you know Christmas is pagan and God is not a Trinity?"

Not only did I not know; I really didn't care! How do you convey this without sounding rude?

I had been to Sunday school once. My experience was troubling. A first impression of religious people in general was their tendency to reduce everything to black and white binaries. I, on the other hand, preferred colors.

Doctrines and theology were not glued to the inside of my thick skull. I was neither offended nor invested in challenging Johnny's bottomless well of surprises. I suspected my buddy was compensating for something or other with all these obsessions. This was a minor flaw like a birthmark; to be ignored while not being *rude by noticing.* But, who am I to judge?

I was pig-ignorant about these matters and it was obviously important to him.

As we became best-best buddies, I grew restless with the interruptions to our equable camaraderie. I was less shy about speaking up, although it was awkward for me to challenge my best friend. Johnny exerted an advantage. Although we were equals, his conversancy with his own religious teachings became trump card in a natural rivalry for the "top dog" status.

Mostly, I didn't "get it." Who spends their waking hours reading up on religious doctrine when it is the 60's and the best time in history to be alive? We lived in interesting times when everything was changing in society. I eventually came to understand no friendship was possible unless Johnny recruited me to his religious worldview. He saw the world as temporary and escape absolutely necessary! In his belief system, the end was near. So, why aim for success or wealth? Why even try? His religion discouraged ambition.

Friendship is based on sharing the same sense of reality and developing close affinities which lead to two-way communication. Once you are on the *receiving only* end problems do occur. I became the cup *poured into* by him. He was Mister hot kettle.

My mother had read to me from the Book of Revelation for some kind of spooky thrill. My Grandfather studied world religions while searching for the *true* one and scribbling copious margin notes in his stacks of books. My Grandmother was a lapsed Catholic with horror stories of life in a convent as a girl. My mother was more into UFO's and Ouija boards than Jesus.

I had never met my Dad. I was incurious about religious matters. They seemed arbitrary, obsessive and tedious.

Religious people I had met gave me the creeps. My best friend's family was not like that. Their house displayed no icons. The kindness and gentleness inside their home was a magnet for me. My own household was dysfunctional on a poisonous emotional level.

To my reckoning, naturally good people were attracted to other good people and that created religion. I never believed religion made so-so people "better."

Johnny wanted to "study the Bible" with me and we set some time aside each week. For me, this was just to "get it over with" because such seemed inevitable. It would be like listening to some dear friend's conspiracy theories.

It turned out Bible study was a polite hoax *as it had been presented.*

Johnny provided a garish, day-glow orange book titled, "From Paradise Lost to Paradise Regained." He explained it was an "aid." Oh-h-h-h, so that's how it's done: 90% "aid" and 10% Bible. I caught on pretty quickly. As long as a scripture was quoted it was *Bible*.

Why not simply say, "We're going to study my religion's ideas and then, we'll look something up in the Bible that may support it." Nope, there was not only certainty attached to these opinions, there was absolute certainty. I'd learn later why they were so confident.

Prefab questions at the bottom of each page, for me to parrot *correct* answers in response, irked me.

I felt this was stifling curiosity. I fought it and asked my own nuisance questions. My friend was exasperated within a couple of weeks of this routine.

You can lead a horse to water…

For one thing, I was skeptical by nature about the way religious people flip Bible pages. If they want to prove something they take a little from here and a little from there and then up and over and down. It was a buffet in a cafeteria and not any kind of context-driven process: a bamboozle method! Not that trickery was a conscious motive on anybody's part. It wasn't.

I absorbed by osmosis many interpretations of the scriptures from constant attendance at their Kingdom Hall. It wasn't called "church." Witnesses had a thing about commonplace Christian words such as church, they did not like them! The strategy was to change familiar religious terms into some *other word.* Jesus died, not on a cross but a *pole* or *torture stake,* for instance. Eventually I caught on. This way of speaking was an insider's language and only another JW would recognize the odd phrase as *Shibboleth.*

Witnesses simply describe their religion as "being in the Truth." When they say "the Truth" they only mean one thing: the Watch Tower Society's *current* opinion.

Think of it as hollowing out a pumpkin and carving a face. You still have the pumpkin and yet it has been transformed to represent Halloween.

My family warned me, "Jehovah's Witnesses twist the scriptures." My reaction to it was, "How would *you* know?"

In fact, their warnings drove me more and more to defend Johnny's beliefs. This was more my evaluation of family than of the Watch Tower gravitas.

How can a non-expert refute an expert? That's how I reckoned it. I was choosing sides little by little by defending my friend. Was I naïve in thinking of him as a Bible expert? Draw your own conclusions.

For many decades the leadership of the JW's insisted it should not be called a religion, just a Society of Bible Students. "Religion," it was opined, consisted only of demon-inspired teachings certain to fail. Later, to acquire tax exempt status, they became a religion and all such pretentious talk pretty much changed. It was flipped into *true* religion vs. *false* religion. Some of the longtime members still refer to their religion as: The Society. Old habits die hard for all of us, myself included.

Johnny and his family chauffeured me 3 times a week to their Kingdom Hall. It was their idea and a kind gift of time and energy and thoughtful outreach. Nothing less was expected of all Witnesses everywhere, I learned.

I confess, I enjoyed my first experience! I overcame my preconceived notions this would be Sunday School. It wasn't like that at all.

Smiling people introduced themselves to me and treated me as though I was interesting and important to them. A cynic might say they were *love-bombing* me. No cynical expression could come across as genuine.

It felt genuine to me. They seemed to need me and it felt great to be a part of a people eager to practice goodness.

I was smiled at and patted on the back and my hand was shaken over and over again. I felt myself emerging little by little from the shy cocoon of reticence I never had been able to overcome before. I was drawn out.

None of this struck me as pretense or fakery. What came out of them was straight from the heart, plain-spoken and relaxing. For all intents and purposes these meetings were so low key you might fall asleep. Some did after a long hard day at work.

We sat on uncomfortable folding chairs inside a plain, rectangular building facing a slightly elevated stage. Worship, as such, was confined to words spoken.

Compared to my earlier Sunday School encounter, the Kingdom Hall was much smaller and had none of the trappings of religion's windows, candles, organ music or robes of service. Children remained with parents for the services which were not called "services." It was just a "meeting." A less worshipful choice of words, I thought.

For all practical purposes this could have been a Loyal Order of Moose lodge meeting! (You've got the questions? We've got the antlers!) Most speakers were like "Farmer Bob" doing his first TV interview. I stifled many a chuckle as affectionate mockery. The amateurish spectacle made you root for the people on the platform. I just wanted them to survive it all.

"Brothers and Sisters, let us commence to begin. Would you take your cheers, please?" (*Chairs, please*). It was entertaining in a charming way. I relaxed guardedness.

These were folksy people I could warmly embrace and learn to love. And I did! Baby steps led me onward.

Did I learn anything useful? Sometimes it seemed like I did. My ears were tickled from hearing slightly off-kilter beliefs expounded with a straight face. Like what?

Beardless Jesus died on a pole, for example. Most Jehovah's Witnesses do not embrace going to heaven—they settle for secondary status on Earth, like a commune of Woodstock hippies living off the confiscated possession of billions of dead people destroyed at Armageddon! Hey, I'm not kidding.

JW's don't actually take *communion*. Once a year they gather to NOT take communion. At "The Lord's Evening Meal," (yet another changeover phrase) you might see an elderly person partaking of the bread and wine. Everybody else just *sits* and rubber-necks the "anointed" partakers. Think about that for a moment.

Earth-bound Witnesses regard the heaven-bound with a spooky fascination. Being "anointed" is analogous to being gay: you *just know,* somehow. If you claim you are—well, how can anybody prove otherwise?

Every baptized Witness knocks on doors and *places* (exchanges for money as a donation) books and magazines with householders. Time spent in total hours must not fall below 10 hours each month.

Reporting stats is essential for a good appearance of glowing spiritual health. This takes on the rubric of a sales quota rather than a spiritual ideal.

The Witness ministry actually consists of an endless stream of "true" teachings which often fizzle. Predictions fail and are replaced. Interpretations change and are retired quietly, ad infinitum.

The rank and file breathlessly awaits New Light emendations like slow-motion news bulletins. *Truth* is the soap opera which never ends, so, stay tuned! If something is true, why change it? If not, why publish it? (You just don't ask *those* questions!)

The official spin is this. Truth is progressive revelation. *Does this make sense?* A dark room with one candle burning is not made progressively brighter by blowing out the old candle and lighting the new one. Progressive knowledge *adds and does not replace.*

Members do not pick and choose which teachings to accept or believe. Go along to get along and smile.

As a Jehovah's Witness, you certainly would NOT celebrate Easter or Christmas, or Thanksgiving or anybody's birthday. Nor would you salute the flag or sing the National Anthem or vote in an election or join the Y.M.C.A. No charities or hospitals are sponsored.

Males are forced to remain beardless with the most peculiar prejudice imaginable. It is a do-as-you-are-told policy. Loyalty is everything, so, *swallow the camel.*

Such contrarian teaching sounded spectacularly weird when I first heard it. But, stick around and make friends and you'll grow accustomed.

Saying the name "Jehovah" stops sounding wonky after a month. Remember the saying? Boil a frog sl-o-w-ly and it won't try to leap from the pot! The group you surround yourself with defines your new "normal" eventually.

The Society owned its own printing presses and the workers didn't have to be paid minimum wage because they had the privilege of working at Bethel, the House of God. The Ministry School was like a self-defense class. Training for Bible-whoop-ass, is what I called it. Plain folks practiced winning every argument or debate. It is like learning to dance by following footprints.

There was never a need to feel "stage fright" in door-to-door work; you had already memorized every possible response to every sort of objection by practicing at the meetings. Practice, they say, makes perfect.

Frederick Franz, the resident sage for almost 80 years, specialized in do-it-yourself Bible Chronology. This was used to predict events and support beliefs. None of the predictions ever proved themselves to be less than disastrous failures. He was rewarded for this by acquiring the Presidency of the Watch Tower Society.

The obsessive passion for home-brew chronology began with William Miller. Miller figured out the world was coming to an end in 1843. (Spoiler: It didn't.) Then, he said it would be 1844. (Wrong again.) The Great Disappointment this was called. You can see why chronology is so appealing to Jehovah's Witnesses as a progressive *rain dance.* Or, can you? It does not follow!

Unfortunately, the foundation of this religion rests entirely on a corkscrew of chronology. Politely ask the next Jehovah's Witness who knocks on your door to explain how the Bible teaches 1914 was the absolute date of the establishment of Jesus' kingdom.

Stare wonderingly and listen to their explanation. How can anybody accept this as incontrovertible? Probably the way I did. I smiled and nodded like I was following all of it. At core, I felt it was my ignorance which made things murky rather than the vapidity of it all. And they say the Trinity doctrine is confusing!

If the Organization printed, spoke or taught anything, the millions of JW's all over the world were obligated to believe it and deliver it fresh to your door!

It all began in Theocratic Ministry School practice session and ended with a transaction on the doorstep. Women could become part of the distribution program and they had proved highly successful. A clever loophole had been carved out of the ironclad rule that women "keep silent" in the congregation.

If you placed them on the platform stage at the front of the Kingdom Hall and let them interact with each other (scripted) the audience is merely eavesdropping! This may be the single most successful innovation in the entire religion. Training women meek, submissive and endearing creates a great distribution advantage.

Did I mention—*unpaid?*

Theocratic Ministry School was a guided do-it-yourself training program where no written exam is necessary. Naturally, nobody ever graduates either.

Miniature sermons are presented by students to other students. (Did you ever see the M.C. Escher drawing of the hand drawing the hand that is drawing itself?)

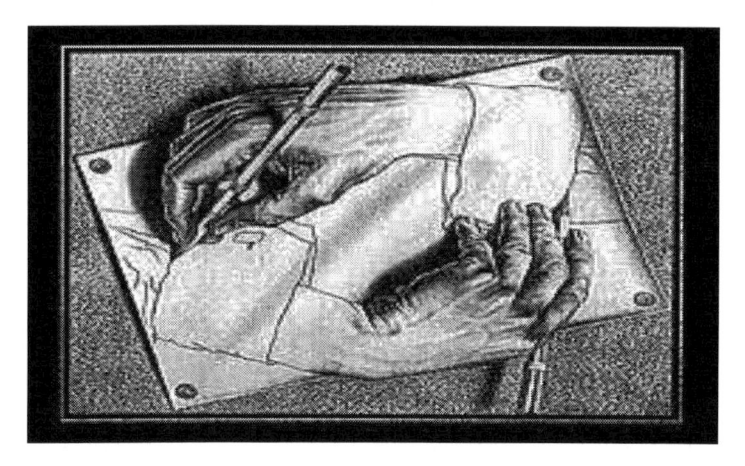

The school elder gives a helpful critique afterward. This school has an arts and crafts atmosphere rather than an academic flavor. It falls far short of accreditation; better than nothing. *Amateur hour* might also be accurate.

I hoped I might acquire an education in public speaking. I might learn argumentation, history and overcoming objections. Compared to a Bible college and a degree in divinity studies, well, there is no comparison!

The essential thing is to sound like you know what you are talking about. Take the wonderful Greek word: *parousia*. In the early days of the religion, the second coming of Jesus was predicted to occur on a certain date—1874. A prediction puts a belief to the test.

The date came and went. Now, your average garden variety Christian might say: "Either Jesus missed his ride or we were wrong about our date."

With the word *parousia*, however, the problem was solved! Some enterprising Bible student discovered there was a secondary definition for the Greek word. By inserting this *other* meaning in place of the usual one; it's an almost magical solution to embarrassment.

This "coming" could flip-flop into "already present!" Got that? Jesus is *already back,* but, you can't see him because he's, um, *invisible!* Never mind trying to follow it. You need to hear it a thousand times to accept it.

With interpretive genius mostly coming across like a mechanic explaining the internal combustion engine; who was I to ask the kind of penetrating question that would expose any obvious flaws? The fact of the matter is: I knew nothing and my teachers appeared to be brilliantly well informed. Peer dynamic can be quite a powerful persuader. I can't say I believed it because it was almost like learning how to do a card trick: functionally fascinating. Where is the "truth" in a card trick? The *effect* is what counts. You achieve by practice.

What makes the card trick so fascinating? You don't know how it is done. You are fooled and that means your powers of observation are defeated. Having the "meaning" of Bible secrets explained is very much like joining the Magician's Union and gaining the power and ability to perform in front of others without revealing the mundane secret: for a trick to work something is always hidden when the other thing is revealed.

This elusive "true" truth is really a horizon line. You continually approach and it is always the same distance ahead. There is no "there" there.

Don't knock it

Higher education might lead to a career and money and security rather than the customary job of JW's everywhere as a janitor, or mobile home builder, window washer, truck driver or roofer.

Witnesses do not remain in good standing if they seek college and career. Why get an education? The world is ending!

Why follow a career path? The world was ending soon. Why save for retirement? The world was ending soon. See?

Non-Jehovah's Witnesses wonder what it must be like to go into a strange neighborhood and wake people up out of a sound sleep. I can't speak for anybody but myself. It was hilarious and tragic. We were angels on their doorstep catching them at their worst.

The awkward way the deer-in-the-headlights listened to our canned sermon was a thing to behold.

Many people would wait to the bitter end when you were displaying the dazzling array of Watchtower plus Awake! then croak: "I'm sorry, I'm not interested."

This door-knocking crew in your neighborhood was there to separate the *sheep* from the goats. If you give us the money and take our books and magazines—guess which one you are? That's right. You are a *sheep-like* one. You are a candidate for life on Paradise Earth.

If you slam the door or give an excuse, we JW's viewed you as one who asks for destruction at Armageddon. Think about that. Our visit is life or death! Such hubris!

Our job as a JW is to start the faux Bible study and place the body snatcher seedpod under your bed and wait for you to fall asleep. You'll wake up wanting to be baptized and rearing to go out and repeat the process virally.

Suffice it to say, I was baptized as a member in November of 1963. At my baptism the feeling I experienced was a sensation of absolutely *nothing.* I thought, "Now I'm obligated. Gee, what have I done?"

I half expected to be inhabited by a pilot light of numinous awakening instead of emptiness. Like a calf that is roped, thrown and branded stands up wondering how it all went so wrong, I can't really explain it to you. To those who understand, no explanation is necessary. To those who don't understand, no explanation is possible! This was expected of me. I dutifully complied.

From the day Johnny and I met until today it has been 54 years. We were 12 and now we are 66!

Would we remain friends if it were not forbidden for him to do so? I don't call myself his spiritual "Brother" any longer, but, I'm still a human being with feelings and memories and a heart full of love for him.

It seems puzzling how Christians who claim to have the unshakable "truth" and power of God behind them are insecure and afraid somebody might say something to destroy the belief that convinced them. Is solid faith really so fragile—or is it the foundational source?

An article published in the July 15, 2011 edition of *The Watchtower* warns JW's to stay clear of "mentally diseased" apostates who should be avoided at all costs.[3]

This is what the official *Watchtower* article spells out, not unlike a Muslim Mullah might pronounce a *fatwa:*

---

[3] Page 16, para 6

"The obligation to hate lawlessness also applies to all activity by apostates. Our attitude toward apostates should be that of David, who declared: 'Do I not hate those who intensely hate you, O Jehovah and do I not feel a loathing for those revolting against you? With a complete hatred I do hate them. They have become to me real enemies.' (Psalm 139:21, 22)...

"Apostates capitalize on errors or seeming mistakes made by Brothers who take the lead. Our safety lies in avoiding apostate propaganda as though it were poison, which in fact it is.—Romans 16:17, 18."[4]

You are either for them by agreeing with every word printed in *The Watchtower* or you are their bitter enemy, so, shut up! Watchtower thinking has no room for nuance or prudent testing. There is no possible way THEY COULD BE WRONG. There is no such thing as the "loyal opposition." What seems lacking is humility!

If your disfellowshipped mother were dying of cancer and she telephoned you for comfort; you could not speak to her or go visit her.

Q: *What would Jesus do?*

A: (Yes, that is a rhetorical question.)

---

[4] *The Watchtower*, July 15, 1992 pp. 12-13 para. 19

Draft Classifications during the Vietnam War

I-A
Available for military service

I-A-O
Conscientious objector available for noncombatant military service only

I-C
Member of the armed forces of the U.S., the Coast and Geodetic Survey, or the Public Health Service

I-D
Member of reserve component or student taking military training

I-H
Registrant not currently subject to processing for induction

I-O
Conscientious objector available for civilian work contributing to the maintenance of the national health, safety, or interest

I-S
Student deferred by statute (High School)

I-Y
Registrant available for military service, but qualified for military only in the event of war or national emergency

I-W
Conscientious objector performing civilian work contributing to the maintenance of the national health, safety, or interest

II-A
Registrant deferred because of civilian occupation (except agriculture or activity in study)

II-C
Registrant deferred because of agricultural occupation

II-D
Registrant deferred because of study preparing for the ministry

II-S
Registrant deferred because of activity in study

III-A
Registrant with a child or children; registrant deferred by reason of extreme hardship to dependents

IV-A
Registrant who has completed service; sole surviving son

IV-B
Official deferred by law

IV-C
Alien

The Holy Grail:

IV-D
Minister of religion or divinity student

IV-F
Registrant not qualified for any military service

*****

Between the time of my baptism in 1963 and the time of my sentencing to Federal Prison was a period of four years.

My life consisted of a clash of worlds. I, like other Jehovah's Witnesses, lived in two worlds. One was real along with the rest of humanity. The other one was supposed to be even more real. The world of Jehovah was the one that needed to matter the most.

This required two minds and two personalities. These two distinct parts of your existence fit inside one another and operated in an amazing and remarkable way: each was invisible to the other and yet both were YOU.

My family had wanted and urged me to go to college and get a good education. I had an almost miraculous talent in art as a natural gift. On the other hand, my religious "family" frowned on education and a career in art as a waste of time because—let's face it—what good would it be? Armageddon was pretext in excluding achievement beyond a subsistence existence.

Really smart JW's developed what I'd call a double-life. They did normal things on the sly and did Witness things for ritual rain-dance purposes.

I don't mean to imply it was a squalid treason of self-serving duplicity. No, it was a kind of social survival. Unless you are brain dead you cannot pretend Armageddon's angels of death are about to pounce on the wicked every minute of every day of your life. For that is what it amounts to: a paralysis of doom.

Hanging on to real world sanity is vital to avoid a pervasive sense of doom and depression day to day.

There is such a thing as *cognitive dissonance.*

You have two compartments. Inside the first compartment you have true belief in your religious faith. In the second compartment you try to have a reasonable life with happiness and accomplishments. When the two clash: you lie to yourself! This could be as innocent as going to a movie that is disapproved. You rationalize and keep it out of view.

Soon my life was confronted with a brick wall and no way around the collision of worlds by a wrecking ball.

The problem with disconfirmation is you cannot and will not act on it because there is no place in your belief system for skeptical disproof. So, you just pretend to see it, but you hide it and never really look at it again.

When Galileo offered to allow Priests to gaze through his telescope they recoiled in horror. Why would any self-respecting believer in the Bible want to do that?

A Jehovah's Witness was asked if he had read former Governing Body elder Ray Franz's expose' of the inner workings of the Watch Tower Society.

He looked horrified as he explained, "Why would I want to read something that might make me lose my faith in my religion?" As if this wasn't the self-same goal of the Witnesses in their own door-to-door ministry! In their view, destroying *other faiths* is perfectly fine.

August 1966

During the Vietnam war 5,000 draft age men turned in their draft cards rather than be conscripted. These were protests. 200,000 men were accused by the Federal Government of being Draft Offenders. 25,000 were indicted. Out of the 25,000, only 8,750 were convicted.

Out of the 8,750 who were convicted, only 4,000 were imprisoned. 4,200 local Draft Boards stayed busy registering, rejecting and selecting men of military age for training and service.

Non-political protest was rare in those times. Mennonites, Quakers and homosexuals were a separate problem for draft boards. Adventists could be medics. Jehovah's Witnesses were a special case.

Every member of the Watch Tower Society was repeatedly assured by their Governing Body they were qualified to be ministers of Jehovah God. Consequently, the males were expected to seek exemption and avoidance of any duty to the Nation in a time of war except preaching the "good news."

Preaching the good news means trading *The Watchtower* and *Awake!* magazines for money as well as offering the latest jaw-breaking title (*Life Everlasting in Freedom of the Sons of God*; *Babylon the Great Has Fallen-God's Kingdom Rules!*) for donation, and, as a special free bonus: a Bible study!

Serving in the military was forbidden, as was alternate hospital or civic duty, and the religion's young men were compelled to seek exemption on the grounds of their identity as ordained ministers.

The bargain was this. If you agreed to spend 100 hours each month going door-to-door and placing books and magazines, the Watch Tower Society would provide you with a letter of official endorsement or *bona fides*. Otherwise, you were on your own to prove you were a minister.

Jehovah's Witnesses, who could scrape up the money, were able to hire the top litigator associated with the Watch Tower Society's Supreme Court cases, whose name was Hayden C. Covington. Ironically, his most high-profile and diligent defense had been conducted on behalf of Cassius Clay aka Muhammad Ali, a non-member.[5]

---

[5] *Jailed for Peace: The History of American Draft Law Violators, 1658-1985* (Contributions in Military Studies), Stephen Kohn. Praegar (1986)

Historical note: Cassius Clay

Six months before I was incarcerated, a high-profile personality drew the world's attention away from the sport of boxing and placed the spotlight on a Nation of Islam's claim of pacifism regarding the Vietnam War.

Heavyweight champion Cassius Clay declared himself to be a Muslim who was changing his "slave" name to Muhammad Ali. Further, Clay/Ali declared to the press he was under no obligation to fight in Vietnam unless Allah commanded him to go.

Ali was first Drafted and rejected in 1964. But by 1966 the Army had lowered its standards of qualification and the athlete was facing eligibility.

Ali refused to take the step forward into military service and found himself convicted of draft evasion with a five-year sentence plus a fine of $10,000. His boxing title was taken away along with his right to future earnings in his profession.

The high-powered Jehovah's Witness attorney, Hayden C. Covington defended Ali because of his record of successes before the Supreme Court defending First Amendment cases.

Muhammad Ali did not have to serve any actual prison time. Covington appealed the case and the boxer was free to lecture at universities and religious gatherings of Muslims to generate public support.

Five years later, the United States Supreme Court ruled 8-0 in the boxer's favor, declaring that Ali had met all three standards for exemption required by law. His original conviction was reversed. The three-step standard meant: war in any form was oppose; his views were religiously founded; the extent of his conscientious objection was a deeply held belief.[6]

---

[6] Source: *On This Day: Muhammad Ali Convicted of Draft Evasion* June 20, 2011 06:00 AM by Denis Cummings.

1966 Draft Board

Six of Fort Worth's leading citizens had responded to an invitation to membership on its Draft Board. The group included the head of the local taxi cab company, a Baptist minister, an attorney, a physician, a construction foreman and shift leader from the Post Office. Draft Board meetings were often chaired by Mr. Charles Needham at the downtown Federal Building.

The members of the group visibly straightened as I entered the room and began inspecting me. My job was to convince them I was a genuine minister of my faith. I was on my own. I was only 19 years old. I *eyeballed* them back.

Each man was studying me intently; making mental notes and categorizing every detail; forming preliminary conclusions about who and what I was as a person and a citizen and maybe as minister. First impression counts.

For one thing, the physician stared at my shoes, which were definitely cheap. My hair was groomed, but, not professionally trimmed. I thought of myself as a young man exuding shopworn elegance. I think I looked homemade.

The Postal clerk studied how I held my body stiffly and how tense my lips made me appear. *This kid is nervous.* That was what they were all probably thinking. I didn't really know. I was experiencing a frisson of paranoia and self-induced manic energy. I was, however, mentally prepared.

The Postal clerk smiled, perhaps remembering his own first day at the Post Office as the only black man among all whites. I was guessing.

He began to sympathize a little, maybe? Wanting to please the Lord did not make you a coward. My imagination ran riot.

Charlie Needham spoke.

"Please sit down and make yourself comfortable. Terry. Is that how you'd like to be addressed?

Needham glanced again at the wall clock and noted the time.

"Terry *is* okay."

I sat in the center of the U shaped tables on the opposite side of the members with my chair pushed out three feet away from the nearest man.

I could see all of them and they could scrutinize me. I felt like a slow swimmer circled by sharks. I'm not saying I was paranoid. I'm just not saying.

"We will now proceed with our hearing. Can you give us a brief Statement covering your request for ministerial deferment?"

Their eyes bore in with expectancy. It really felt like a firing squad listening for the order to "fire!"

I cleared my throat again and again as I spoke. My mouth was dry. I was articulate. My vocabulary was unusually broad and detailed. I was *odd duck.*

As the self-help nerd who had often spent many hours memorizing large lists of words for fun; the kid these men were listening to must have puzzled them.

I repeated to the Draft Board the essential points I had already confided to the F.B.I. agents who interviewed me the month before: Who, what, when, where, how and *why* I am who I am. They were looking for authenticity.

F.B.I. agents had been keen to know how long my association with Jehovah's Witnesses had been developing. I explained I had been more or less attending the Polytechnic Kingdom Hall since I was 12 years old. That had been 1959. I became a baptized member in 1963. They scribbled it all down and departed. Now, I repeated it all for the local Draft Board.

I explored each man's face as I spoke using all the highly developed *skills* I'd been absorbing at the Kingdom Hall in Theocratic Ministry School of Fort Worth. I made excellent eye contact and used persuasive gestures and modulated my voice well as I present the summation. I was an actor in my role as theologian. Besides, there was a scripture about being "a theatrical spectacle to men."

Morris Culpepper loosened the top button on his shirt and undid his tie just enough to prevent strangulation. Rubbing his neck, he started scribbling with a yellow pencil on a legal pad. He was taking his job seriously, for sure.

"Here is what I want to know. Do you have a regular job? Do you work for a living? Or, do you preach in a church like normal preachers?"

He angled his massive head toward Reverend Oakes to indicate *normal.*

"I am a portrait artist and self-employed. I don't punch a clock anywhere. I live at home with my grandparents and mother. Jehovah's Witnesses are ministers; all of us. We're the ones ringing your doorbell on the weekends while you're trying to sleep."

I managed a wry smile as Reverend Oakes pouted at my unseemly lack of seriousness.

"What we mean is this," Oakes tapped his manicured fingers together in the spider-doing-push-ups hand gesture.

"Are you a full-time minister so you actually deserve deferment?"

Oakes was confrontational without being mean-spirited.

This was a question I'd never been asked before.

"Well, our ministry is something we all take seriously enough that we don't just wait for Sunday."

"You consider yourselves Christians and not *Jehovah's*?" Oakes inquired archly.

"We say, Jehovah's *Christian* Witnesses."

Oakes twitched his mouth with a dismissive grunt and turned to his left.

Attorney Parks was fidgeting in his uncomfortable oak chair. He pulled a *Mont Blanc* pen from his inside suit pocket and pointed it like the muzzle of a Derringer pistol toward me.

"Correct me, please, if I state this improperly. My understanding is Jehovah's Witnesses won't perform alternate service in a hospital as community service even as a privilege extended to persons like you."

"Yet, if the Judge compels you by sentence to perform the same service you had refused; you happily comply and take the job! I have to say this makes no logical sense in my legal experience."

Parks narrowed his dark brown eyes and seemingly forced himself not to blink as he awaited my answer. I felt like he was a snake trying to hypnotize a mouse. I was more dazzled by his sharkskin suit and expensive fountain pen.

"To accept alternate service to military service is to substitute this for that. This violates our Christian neutrality. It is like taking an I.O.U. for money owed.

"It means the same. So, I have to refuse. But, if the Judge makes it compulsory rather than voluntary, as dutiful Christians under subjection we comply."

Attorney Parks raised his eyebrows and chortled.

"Excuse me, you aren't the Swiss. You have no neutrality. Caesar is Caesar in both instances. The military *and* the Judge work for Caesar. It's six of one and a half-dozen of the other. You are confused."

"Seventh-day Adventists refuse even to pick up a rifle but one of them during WWII won the Medal of Honor saving lives under fire as a medic on the battlefield. You think you're too good for that? Neutral doesn't cut it. It is a contrived position and illegal."

Reverend Oakes, Charlie Needham and I each started speaking at the same time. Needham paused and let the Reverend take the lead while holding his hand up to me as a "stop" sign.

"Thank you, Charlie. I want to say this to you, young man…"

Oakes took on the fervor of the actor John Carradine in the film *Grapes of Wrath*. His craggy countenance waggled with melodramatic intensity as though mugging for an unseen camera.

"The Pharisee binds people with burdens of self-invented rules, regulations, traditions and twisted reasoning. Jesus said it burdens the faithful unnecessarily but, in stark contrast, his yoke was light upon your shoulders…"

Needham jumped in at the pause.

"We aren't here for religious debate or legal harangue; we just want some simple statements of fact for our decision. I hope you understand."

I sighed and shook my head as the Reverend shot him a disappointed look.

Culpepper wasn't following any of the fancy arguments. He lost the thread early on, it was obvious.

"Son, what if everybody believed the same way you did?"

Now here was a straight line I could volley!

"There would be no wars; no need for a Draft Board and we wouldn't be sitting here today."

I relaxed feeling I had finally scored a point. Yet, I was troubled by what had just been said by the attorney. Culpepper wasn't having in one-ups by this smart kid.

"What I mean is. . .what if only Americans believed just as you do and the Communists *knew* that?"

This was going to be easy. . .

"I suppose you could say we'd all being doing exactly what Jesus commanded by turning the other cheek and loving our enemy!"

Charlie Needham's sense of propriety now violated; he addressed the subject in a more serious way than before.

"Son, if somebody broke into your house and threatened your family's life, wouldn't you defend them with violence if it saved their lives?"

"Sir, the Vietnamese people have not broken into my house. If anything, my country has trespassed into their huts."

I suddenly had a sense I was in a riptide but the words came to me easily.

Culpepper stiffened. He looked like his heart was pounding double time.

"My father served in WWII because the Japanese bombed Pearl Harbor. He wasn't going to let Emperor Hirohito or Adolf Hitler or Benito Mussolini take over this world or run his country."

"We'd all be under Hitler's thumb or going up in smoke in some Auschwitz if God-fearing Americans all believed the way you *Jehovah's* believe."

Culpepper's eyes were bulging out of his skull and he seemed to know he was not comporting himself well. This was passionate patriotism overcoming him.

I took a deep breath and answered thoughtfully and in whatever measured tones I could summon.

"Jehovah's Witnesses died in concentration camps in WWII. One thing you can be certain of. No Jehovah's Witness ever pointed a rifle at your father or pulled the pin on a hand grenade in the armies of Hitler, Mussolini or Hirohito."

It was a prudent answer. I thought it cut to the heart of his objections.

Doctor Jarvis appeared to feel the heat of argument was getting off point and the clock was running out as well. He glanced at his watch *and* the clock.

A change of subject might cool things down enough to wind things to a close.

"Would you say Jehovah's Witnesses cherish life and view it as a sacred gift from God?"

Jarvis was laying a subtle trap rather obviously, I thought.

"Sometimes, if you save your life you lose it in a greater sense."

Jarvis leaned forward as a knight about to unseat a rival in a joust.

"If life is so precious to you; why do you allow little children to die rather than accept a blood transfusion?"

I cringed inwardly. This was the most difficult issue to explain. Especially with doctors who took a black and white view of life, it was hard to argue persuasively. To me, it made no practical sense either—yet, the Bible confused me on this.

"Our hands are tied by what the scriptures say. Nobody wants a child to die under any circumstance. We believe the life is in the blood and it is sacred."

Culpepper's body jerked like he'd been stung by a wasp.

"Any religion that stands by and lets an innocent child die—when they *could* be saved by a doctor—is no religion I'd care to call Christian. That's pure evil!"

"Well, it's in the Hebrew and Greek Testaments, Sir. We didn't put it there. We just obey it. 'Keep yourselves free of blood.' Make of it what you will."

I was out of my depth on this. I couldn't understand what any of this questioning had to do with my own deferment. Every denomination has deep teachings hard to bear. Needham looked like he had had enough for his own decision. It was up to him to bring order and organization and accomplish what they set out to do to conclude matters straight away.

"I think we've all heard enough to determine what we are dealing with here. You can have the last word if you like, in summation."

It felt like a high tide had crashed on my head and I struggled back to the surface. What could possibly change any minds?

"Gentlemen, thank you for taking the time and trouble to hear me out. When I was a kid I wanted nothing better than to be a jet pilot in the Air Force."

"I played army and cowboy and owned a two gun holster. I was an ordinary, normal American kid. Gradually, by studying with Jehovah's Witnesses, I came to see my service to God from a different line of view. That's why there isn't just one church, I guess. There are thousands of them and we all differ in some way."

"Logically, they can't all be true and right. So, we have a standoff and the freedom to step on one side of the line or the other and make our best call. I request a deferment to tell Jehovah's side of the story. I can't take up weapons in good conscience and I can't work in a hospital for reasons I explained. Conscience compels me. I am just trying to do the right thing."

If anything, my words were coming from somewhere deep inside of me. This was sincere confession. It was a command performance and self-conscious.

I believed what I said. I had been carefully taught. It was my duty. I never mentioned I'd been coached.

Charlie Needham nodded as though putting a period at the end of a long sentence with his chin.

"Thank you. We'll confer and give our decision directly to proper authorities. You'll get something in the mail eventually from the Selective Service concerning your status. That's about it."

I clutched my green New World Translation of the Bible as I quickly departed from the room and down the staircase to the lobby and out into the bright sunlight. I took in a deep breath and tried to clear my head.

First, there had been an F.B.I. interrogation and now, this. When would it all end? I was almost certainly going to end up in prison no matter what I said. I groaned.

Exhaling slowly and fighting off a gnawing sense of panic, I set off walking to the bus stop. Inside of a few months the die would be cast.

Later, arrested and released on my own recognizance, I entered the last phase before things got *really* serious.

When a young man is on the threshold between adolescence and adulthood, in a normal context, his life is filled with glorious plans for the future.

There were no such plans for my life which could be immediately realized with any confidence or optimism.

My best friend Johnny got married in 1967 to a young Witness girl who couldn't have been more than 14 or 15 years old. He had a job driving a truck and was already well on his way to an average life and family. Being married, he didn't go for full-time door-to-door ministry. He later told me, he knew how to *play the game.*

I had recently met a Witness girl my age at one of our frequent religious conventions. She had the same heritage as I did: Finnish. She and I tried to make promises to each other about staying in touch in the event of my incarceration, as though that were really going to happen. All sense of *possibility* was dying inside me.

When you have a concrete wall blocking your view of the future something poisonous seeps in to your sense of life itself.

How many young men do you know who have a self-belief to go with their dreams and plans? I didn't.

My personal ambition became stunted and deformed instead of blossoming into reality. The uneasy brooding of *status quo* ruled. It was a countdown.

COURT-APPOINTED ATTORNEY

At my Preliminary Hearing I asked Judge Leo Brewster if I could defend *myself* rather than have an attorney represent me. Judges don't like that sort of thing. It leaves a conviction open to a Writ of Error too easily. Judge Brewster denied my request and appointed attorney George Petrovich.

Reluctantly, I made an appointment and arrived at the law office to discover rows of black and white photographs of aircraft carriers, destroyers and other military depictions decorating his walls. How encouraging!

I heaved the kind of sigh the Burmese tiger heaves when the ground gives way beneath him and he finds himself in a deep pit unable to escape.

George Petrovich was what you'd call an unassuming fellow, which is to say he asked simple, almost naïve questions, and seemed genuinely puzzled why any young man would avoid the military.

"Why are you refusing induction?"

The office was small and the attorney had two chairs set up for us. We faced each other and for some silly reason I kept checking his knee so no accidental contact was made. I had an aversion to physical contact, you see.

I confess I was a bit paranoid because of an incident with the physician who had privately examined me for possible military exemption. I had a bilateral inguinal hernia which this doctor said he could not detect!

And then, he began casually handling my penis *appraisingly* and pretending there were tiny traces of stitches from circumcision remaining which he needed to remove! My circumcision had occurred 19 years earlier. Well, color me suspicious!

He repeated a few times, 'Any other ideas how you might obtain an exemption?' I set a new land speed record exiting his office. The only thing that got blown was my exemption.

Without a medical exemption my only alternative was refusal of induction leading to arrest and now consultation with a court-appointed attorney; the one with his knee a few inches from mine. I figured I needed to stifle my paranoia and emphasize my average Joe-ness. I spoke.

"The military was not the historic choice of Christians trying to obey the teachings of Christ Jesus."

Now, out of what I had just spoken, what part of that puzzled him the most, do you suppose?

"Why'd you say it backwards?" he asked.

"Say what-backwards?"

"You said, *Christ* Jesus, instead of Jesus Christ."

"Well, Christ is a title, like *King* George. You wouldn't say George, King would you?"

It was probably at that moment I saw the light of amicable solidarity fade in the attorney's eyes. He didn't argue. He pulled back physically a bit and simply regarded me quietly. He was wearing a rumpled suit that didn't look tailored or expensive. This guy was losing his hair but had made no effort to hide it with a swooping comb-over. He was a decent, average man.

"So...how do you think I can help you with this, uh... problem? Didn't anybody explain to you that you are not required by the law to actually engage in combat? Alternate service is provided for conscientious objectors. The word "alternate" means other than, as in other than military."

"They've assigned you to Terrell State Hospital right here in Texas. It could have been a lot worse. It could have been out of State, you know."

Here he was like a modern day Galileo reasoning with the Vatican. He wanted me to snap out of my delusion, I could tell. I wanted to, believe me.

"It may be unusual but, I assure you it is a simple Bible principle. No man can serve two masters and I dedicated my life at baptism to one master the Bible identifies as Jehovah." I explained.

"I'm dedicated to ministering door-to-door. That's how Jehovah's Witnesses do their evangelizing—door-to-door." I sported my best winning smile.

Petrovich brightened. He could solve my problem for me; I could see it coming a mile off.

"Look, you can still go door-to-door—in Terrell after work, or even before work. You don't have to live in the hospital. You can easily perform Community Service like a regular 8-5 job—see?" He beamed.

I wanted to tell him not to cloud the issue with facts but he was, after all, an attorney. *Plan B commenced.* I had to enlarge the scope of my defense with historical precedent. Any lawyer would immediately see precedent as binding.

"Back in the 1st century, the early Christians refused to share certain duties of Roman citizens. The Christians felt it a violation of their faith to enter civil or military service. They would not hold political office. They would not worship the emperor. Why? They were subject to Jesus' command. They obeyed God as ruler rather than men."

I didn't even try to guess what he was thinking. I didn't have to, he told me.

"Terry, nobody is asking you to be a Roman citizen. Nobody is forcing you onto the battlefield. Nobody is demanding you become a politician or worship President Johnson. All anybody is asking you to do—since you are opposed to fighting—is do your share by working in a hospital.

It is community service and *not* military service. Why can't an obviously bright guy understand that?"

I *did* get it. Rocket science, it wasn't. It was basic fairness. I took out the verbal trowel and slopped it on.

"Back during the Civil War conscientious objectors were sometimes offered an alternative to fighting in a regiment under the command of an officer."

"They could hire somebody to fight as a substitute. It seemed perfectly fair to the lawyers who thought that up. But, the problem is, it didn't solve the problem. The real problem was the *serving* part. Substituting one thing for another thing which accomplishes the same end is a compromise of integrity as a Christian. That's why hiring a killer is wrong."

My underpaid, court-appointed attorney looked at his wristwatch and shrugged. He spoke musingly.

"I had a roommate in law school. He was an Orthodox Jew. On the Sabbath he wasn't allowed to operate machinery, answer a phone, push an elevator button or anything. It was a 'day of rest' from all physical work. So, you know what he did? He did what all the other Orthodox Jews did in law school. He paid his *goyim* friends to answer the phone and take a message, push the elevator button and drive him where he needed to go. His conscience was perfectly clear."

"Are Jehovah's Witnesses just showing off their super-piety *one-ups*, or what?"

"Well Sir, I appreciate your confusion. I'm not the one to judge. But, suffice to say, we view alternate service in the very same wheelhouse as military service because it involves this-for-that. So, I cannot do it."

The lawyer flashed a momentary pout with his mouth and shrugged it off.

"Okay, fine. How do I plead your case for you then?"

"I guess the most honest way to plead is 'Guilty' and make a plea for leniency for conscience sake. The mitigating circumstance is I'm not doing any wrong by trying to do what is right. You shouldn't punish a twenty year old for trying to serve God according to a clean conscience. That's not justice."

CONVERSATIONS WITH MYSELF

I've often wondered what I might say to myself if I were to meet the younger version of me. What if that were actually possible? Would I bother trying to change my own mind so as to avoid future mistakes by tampering in the past?

Could I prevent my young self from taking the wrong steps? Could I say, "Go ahead and accept hospital work as alternate service?" Wouldn't that mean I'd be disfellowshipped? Yes, I suppose so. Then, prison would not have to happen. But, I never saw that as a choice. I would have lost all my friends. Or, should I say *so-called* friends?

O.T. (Old Terry)   **Y.T.** (Young Terry)

O.T. Hey! Wait up! I know you. I know you like I know myself.

Y.T. I have a good memory for faces. I don't know you.

O.T. This is going to sound weird. I'm actually YOU, only older. Time warp!

Y.T. (Thoughtful pause, then, playing along) You mean I'm going to be ugly?

O.T. Let's not get personal! I have important things to discuss. Okay?

Y.T. If you are me, only older, there can be no *surprises* for you.

O.T. There is much each of us can learn; especially you.

Y.T. I'm still in shock. I take pretty good care of myself by exercising...

O.T. Ah—ha—yeah! I remember that!

Y.T. Obviously something goes awry with that plan!

O.T. How about we avoid obsessing on the physical!

Y.T. Easy for you, for me, difficult!

O.T. What time of life is it for you right now?

Y.T. It's my last year at Morningside Junior High school.

O.T. You have met the kid with freckles and dark red hair already, then.

Y.T. You mean Johnny? Yeah. He's my best buddy.

O.T. (continuing...) I bet he just rode up to you on his bicycle one day and...

Y.T. Yeah. I'm starting to believe this might not be a joke after all—and it's creepy.

O.T. No. Not a joke. Tell me about Johnny. Why is he your best buddy?

Y.T. You already know, obviously.

O.T. I prefer facts uncolored by distortions of time.

Y.T. O.K. Johnny is intelligent and curious and seems to know about subjects I never took an interest in, so, I learn from him. His family takes me to their religious meeting at their Kingdom Hall.

O.T. I notice you said "their" Kingdom Hall. It isn't *yours* yet?

Y.T. I'm not a member. No.

O.T. The Kingdom Hall isn't too churchy?

Y.T. You couldn't drag me into church! Jehovah's Witnesses are very down-to-earth people.

O.T. What does that mean to you? What's the attraction?

Y.T. I've got friends now. Harry, Quincy, Marshall, Johnny. Say, do you suffer amnesia or something?

O.T. Just to be clear on this; you aren't going for spiritual reasons, then?

Y.T. It's more like math class. Kingdom Hall is ordinary, not spiritual pretense and praising the Lord.

O.T. How it can be religious and not spiritual, that's what I'm asking you about…

Y.T. I wonder where you are going with all this.

O.T. That's what I'm wondering about you. What do you want out of it?

Y.T. Why complicate it? I've got friends who don't swear, act tough, or pursue self-destructive activity. That just happens to be the way *I* am.

O.T. Here's a curve ball for you. What about the doctrines and dates and predictions of the end of the world? Does any of that sound true?

Y.T. Is this some kind of loyalty test you are giving me?

O.T. The fish sees the worm and not the hook. That's all I'm saying.

Y.T. Thanks, Confucius. Well, I would venture to say somebody has to have the truth, don't they?

O.T. Why say THE truth? Why are you being so black and white?

Y.T. Now, why don't I ask you what this is really all about? *Tell* me.

O.T. I'm happy to do so. This religion is not going to make you a better human being. You already are a fine young man. You see only the possibilities for good. You don't see the danger. You are going to be wasting the most valuable time you'll ever have to establish a life for yourself. Human opinion disguised as black and white "truth" will land you in prison and cheat you out of an education.

Y.T. Great! I'm in a debate with a heretic and guess who it is? Me!

O.T. Just keep doing what you're doing and you'll end up with nothing.

Y.T. Sounds like you are predicting I'm a failure at everything I ever do.

O.T. Listen to me, you *succeed* at *failing* at everything you do and end up in prison.

Y.T. Why would I go to prison if I'm such a "righteous" kid?

O.T. You will not accept alternate service to the military and that violates Federal law. There is no legitimate reason for that. You'll be following willful manipulation and it will put you in the worst danger imaginable.

Y.T. Wait, stop! That's all I want to hear. If I don't break faith or compromise integrity, why would that be a waste of my time or a waste of my whole life or be dangerous?

O.T. Credible faith is humble and doesn't claim to know it all. You are about to have your faith tested but what really happens is you are testing the truth about Jehovah as taught by men of rigid *opinions*.

Y.T. You're wasting your time—our time. Are we about finished here?

O.T. Finished? I was *finished* the day I came up out of the baptism water. In fact, we both were.

*****

I spoke to my eldest son, Jason, after he read the manuscript for this book. He told me he felt like screaming at Young Terry: "Just accept the alternate service; what's the big deal?" This is an important element in my story and he picked up on it right away.

As you will discover in Part II, the refusal of the legal alternative was an arbitrary *policy* created by the second president of the Watch Tower Society; the most extreme, absolutist stance humanly possible. Most church denominations don't force members to agree with their leaders on matters of personal conscience. Jehovah's Witnesses were handed their *conscience* from policy as a replacement. Choice vanished and loyalty replaced it.

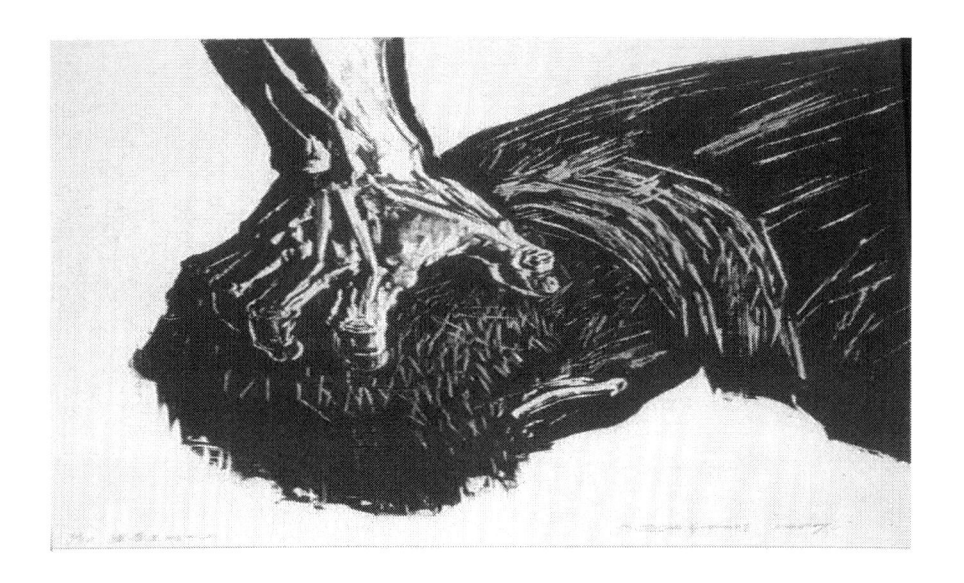

Was anybody holding my head and forcing me to do something I didn't want to do? Of course not.

If you understand nothing else, try to understand this one thing. In *this* religion, like a marriage, you bind and intertwine your life in such a way your own personal preferences fade to second place. Your commitment and your loyalty define you among your peers.

Loyalty to the Governing Body is more important than a simple choice of right or wrong. Loyalty: friend-or-foe identification affects everything. They may be wrong but, in the long run, you simply accept it. Why? So much trust has been placed in the bona fide authority that these men *are being used* by Jehovah. It is no different than a child who trusts his parent even though what is being asked sounds far-fetched. You simply shrug and do as you are told in total trust.

By going along to get along I was facing the wrecking ball.

SUNK-COST FALLACY

Smart people do things for good reasons. When the good reasons run out—what then? We go on trust.

If our trust is betrayed—what then?

We go on loyalty and hope and faith. When blind faith and loyalty destroy our well-being—what then?

Sunk-Cost Fallacy kicks in.

You say to yourself, **"I've already come this far and I can't quit now."** This is fallacious because it is illogical.

Throwing good money after bad in any investment leads to ruin. Gambling addiction strings you along. Religious addiction works the same way.

Religious certainty has no Plan B. It is *all* or *nothing.*

The battered wife often says, "Where else can I go?" When you are trapped and choose to stay—you lose.

(*Fallacies and Argument Appraisal* by Christopher W. Tindale Cambridge University Press 2007)

1967 LESSON NUMBER ONE

(County Jail 6th floor October 23rd)

Twenty in the cage and every man is finishing a hand-rolled cigarette or lighting up a new one. This one is standing. That one is leaning. Haggard white-haired men slam dominoes on metal tables hurling constant swears. Others hunker down and dawdle as though waiting on waiting itself. Their cautious eyes dart and flicker over me. Silent calculations, information for later use on some invisible score sheet, are underway.

Cheap tobacco odor mixes with the scent of sweaty men. I can't help but recoil and listen to the toilet flushing and the grunts and swooshing swirl.

At first, my mind is stunned; a gnawing headache crawls around the shadows in my brain. Cold fear and claustrophobia are companions now.

Angry voices spew profane repetitions: '*mutha fukah* this and *mutha fukah* that', played on an endless loop. Immersion in a filthy world is a new baptism and I'm born anew to life in a man-made hell.

I'm too shocked to look away! Are these wretched grubs and maggots or just the rotting souls of fools? Is this sewer just the smell of waste or is it wasted men?

Is this a rotten joke or what?

Then, slowly, I remember as I'm coming to my senses. I'm supposed to be a Christian who loves his fellow man, who claims he wants to choose this house of pain. And why did I choose this? People I trust said it was the only place I *could* choose and be regarded as obedient.

Jail is not so much a "plac*e*." Jail is where people are *mis*placed.

Recalibrate your sense of time!

Seconds are the heartbeat of a minute dying s-l-o-w-ly. Minutes are an hour in a world you never leave. I see no clocks because time is all there is.

Lesson one: Never pull time. Let it pull you.

How can I really place you in there with me and *make it feel more real*? Let's try this:

First, put away your cellphone and your laptop and turn off your TV. Throw out comfort: no chairs or couches or a bed with mattress. Get rid of your kitchen, groceries, restaurants, snacks or candy. You cannot drive your car. You will not go outside. You cannot turn off the lights. Day and night look the same in a crowded room with people who have nothing to say that interests you. Conversation is impossible.

There are no friends or family. You won't see the face of a baby or a child or woman for years! County jail is a grave where the corpses still blink!

Noise never ends and you'll learn to sleep when you're too exhausted not to. There is no color and there will be no beauty or music or art; only what you've stored in your own heart before you walked inside. Okay? Have I made it clear enough? It isn't TV jail or movie jail.

Jail is leaning on hard surfaces for hours at a time and squatting without new thoughts for days on end. Jail is trying not to breathe while breathing just enough to stay alive. Jail is living at the bottom of the drain with matted hair and spit and rotten teeth.

Jail is for cheaters, thieves and molesters, bullies, sober drunks and dangerous creeps. There is no safe distance or personal space or intermission to the s-t-r-e-t-ch-ing elasticity of time.

Jail is not for 20 year old virgin Christian boys who never hurt a fly. So, why do I think God wants me in here? I mean, *really?* Am I supposed to persuade somebody here of something?

Thought: why were all of my Jehovah's Witness buddies outside enjoying their lives while I'm the only one mucking it up in a concrete and steel toilet bowl called Tarrant County Jail?

Did they not register for the draft in the first place? Was I the only one who did? Am I stupid? Are they smarter than I am for doing what I was told?

Every three days jumpsuits in a bundle are pushed through a hatch from the outer corridor into one gigantic, random heap on our filthy floor.

Sizes vary small-to-average. Nothing is there for fat or tall. Suddenly, I wanted very badly to be average.

Rush and grab. Grab and snatch. Pull off the old and out through the hatch. Twenty naked men stink up an already stinking cell. Pull it on, zip it up and walk away.

I get the final grab. I stripped and pulled and it would not fit! You may as well stuff a giraffe in a gunny sack.

Of course, I'm too tall. The seam cuts into my groin compelling me to stoop. For the first time in my twenty years of life, being six feet four is a painful disadvantage.

Worst of all, there is no way to wash your body clean. There is no shower. We steep in filth. A mop is tossed in once a day with Pine-sol. Whoopty-frickin-do!

There is no toothbrush or razor or soap but there are 20 men and there is one toilet! Let me introduce this metal toilet: it has no toilet seat! But, it does have one handy attachment. It is called your water fountain, a miracle of engineering genius.

Where else in this crazy world but in county jail can one man take a dump while another man takes a refreshing sip of water? The inventor was scathingly genius.

Are you modest? Give that up before it is ripped out of you by necessity!

Letting-bowels-loose with 19 people screaming: "Flush, dammit" afflicts your mind. A man learns to time the flush to the millisecond: not too soon and never too late.

I felt like the bombardier on the Enola Gay.

When I can't hold off one minute longer I unzip my coverall jumpsuit and drop to the metal toilet with fiendish concentration. An inmate yells at me: "Put some *mutha fucken* water behind it!" That is what I do. My Zen moment comes as the toilet, the water, the cell, the universe and I become one. Ah, bliss!

The cell is a room of hard surfaces and constant noise and pungent odors which never go away. Once a day the clanging door opens and an officer calls out a name. One of us exits and a new face is brought in. The population remains at twenty. One day I'll process out. Soon, I hope.

One new guy, as it turns out, is an ex-prizefighter from Jamaica. He has a disgusting skin condition. My hysterical guess was leprosy. Sure, that was unlikely. But, really, was anything unlikely at this point in my life? He immediately asked for butter to rub on his flesh.

He was a swarthy man with white scaly patches on his arms and shoulders. This man scratched constantly and the skin flakes would drift off like a blizzard around him. He was a human snow flurry. "Gimme butter, Mon!" His name was Nat. (None of us had any butter.)

Nat glanced about with wild eyes and walked right up to the smallest guy in the cell. Nat violated this fellow's personal space, you might say. This was a clear breach.

Nat's hair dangled in loose dreadlocks looking like those corks on strings on Australian hats intended to keep flies out of the face.

Nat spoke in a brittle *patois.* His dreadlocks danced.

"Trade licks *wit* me, Mon."

The entire dayroom suddenly perked up.

Game

The Jamaican wedged in close and explained the simple proposal to the diminutive inmate.

1st Haul off and punch Nat on his extremely bulging bicep with your fist as hard as you can.

2nd Nat will haul off and punch your scrawny bicep with his powerful giant-knuckled fist in response!

Scrawny Dude swallowed hard and shrugged a bit. The young man was no more than 25. He probably stole a car or got caught with marijuana. Jail was a place he'd been before. I could intuit he knew he couldn't beg off.

He knew he couldn't walk away or laugh off Nat's challenge. So, he measured the distance with his arm. He fired off what I'd call a "buddy" punch. It seemed to say, "We're the best friends ever, now can I please go home?"

Nat did not appreciate this gesture of international goodwill. "Awwww, Mon, you can do much, much better *dan dat.*"

"Really hit me dis time; go on—I give you first turn again. Go first."

Little Dude pursed his lips, closed his eyes like he was bidding earth goodbye. He drew back and let fly with a solid *smack* on Nat's bowling-ball-sized arm muscle. I'd give it a 10 on the suicide scale. Nat smiled with pretext.

The boxer stood straight, bounced on his legs and took aim, let loose with a bone-cracking jab that sent a tsunami of white hot pain into little Dude's anterior deltoid. Every inmate's sphincter slammed shut.

To his credit as a man, the little Dude took it like a good sport.

Sure, he went white in the face and remained wobbling with a pasted-on smile but, unlike myself, he wasn't looking terrified and hopeless.

Nat spoke. "Okay, Mon—let's go again. Best out of ten wins." Wins? What did that even mean? It was sadism.

I explored prayer...for myself as I edged to the farthest corner of the cell and tried to condense my body into the size of a dust mote.

I withdrew. I withered. I evaded *being.*

Rack Time

Later that evening, at about 9:00 pm the cell door to our Day Room scraped open. It was a passage to a side wall of 5 cells with doors open. We were 4 men to each of the 5 cells. Once the row of doors slam snugly closed the only alternative was to climb onto a metal shelf. This was the sleeping berth. Rack time!

I didn't fit because my sleeping shelf was 6 feet long. I curled my knees into a fetal position facing the metal wall. None of us had a pillow. Each of us was allotted an ironic "bath" towel. (There is no shower facility, remember?)

The only way to fashion a make-shift pillow is to roll up the towel. I rested my head on my own arm and allowed my other arm to drape across my head so my wrist was blocking the light from my eyes. Lights aren't dimmed because that would be humane. Jailors would say they need to keep an eye out for trouble. Nobody watches. We are left to our own personal jungle.

Before "rack time" I was approached by the little guy. His name, he said, was Charles and his left arm looked like purple sausage; Nat's handiwork. Ten blows had left him anything but the winner of the cruel game he'd played.

He asked me to switch cells with him. I said I had better not since I had been specifically assigned to one and that was that. He went from one man to the next with his same plea. Nobody agreed to the trade. *Something was awry.*

Later that night I learned exactly what fate I escaped by my refusal to swap cells with Charles. I heard Charles' muffled, frantic begging and sobbing as he was being *punked*. It was humiliating domination and abuse.

Nat's distinctive voice washed into my cell and condemned my conscience. Charles begged and gave it up. All I thought was, "That could have been me."

Don't ask me about *punked*. You don't want to have that in your head, do you?

Some place inside of a human being is where the *person* resides. It must remain inviolable or the *person* ceases to exist. It is the citadel of integrity. You only give it up to survive. Then, the actual man is gone for good.

You may see him walking around later, but, I assure you, these are dead men inside.

Where once there was a person there is now a scar impersonating him.

As you listen to a man's *soul* being ripped from his body and know how easily it could have been you…I mean, what are you supposed to *do* with that?

Day by day, for ten days, I found myself mentally beseeching my brain's construct of "Jehovah." I recited the list of "Fruits of the Spirit" while asking myself how each of them applied to my present state.

Analytically, the solution was obvious: my sense of doom was being fed to me by my values. If I amended those values by a kind of emergency directive, I could relax my adrenal glands and adapt, accept and advance.

I'm now sure this is where I fully transitioned from a non-spiritual, weak-believer into a True Believer.

TRANSFER

The difference between county lock-up and the transfer to federal minimum security is evolutionary in magnitude. For ten days I had dwelt with prehistoric conditions red with fang and claw. Then, just like the snap of a finger, my name was called and I made my way out of the cell on the sixth floor to a holding cell where I was given my street clothes. In a matter of mintues I went from Neanderthal to *homo sapien* again.

Two sheriff's deputies drove me all the way from Fort Worth to the other side of Dallas. Seagoville prison would be my new "home." To torment me, they told me I was being taken to a miltary prison where I would probably be beaten up regularly for being a coward. For some reason, I didn't believe a word of it. I acted casual and they finally gave up. I had spoiled their fun.

The sunlight and fresh air were too thrilling! The feel of riding in a car was wonderful. Clouds, a landscape, children—it was incredibly moving and I wept silently.

SEAGOVILLE

The sheriff's deputies pulled up in front of the administration building. We three exited and I caught my first glimpse of the facility.

Seagoville is minimum security. Every man works at something. There are no slackers. The routine helped.

Prisoners lived in cell-rooms with a bed, table, chest of drawers and a lamp. The compound itself was built in 1938 as a women's detention center. Imagine a Depression Era architect endeavoring to craft a reformatory atmosphere.

Each new inmate was *uniformed* with war surplus khakis. My hair was buzz-cut like a recruit. Our shoes were army regulation black. (We were required to shine them.) We made our own beds with tight hospital corners. This was daily inspected and enforced!

Each inmate who arrives at this federal facility is tested and interviewed. Your *skillset* is evaluated. A work assignment is matched to your level of intelligence. Exception: If you were a clueless JW who gave the wrong answer back to a superior officer. *Yes, that's me.*

I had the temerity to correct the officer's *understanding* of the "cowardice" of conscientious objectors. "It seems to me, Sir, it is the coward who runs off to Canada and not the fellow who faces the punishment." The Corrections Officer didn't like to be corrected, apparently. I didn't realize he was ex-military. I had never lived around authority in the rigid way it was practiced by bureaucracy. You speak when spoken to and definitely must request permission to speak freely.

The officer told me the results of my test. My I.Q. was just below Average. It was 99. *I smiled suspiciously.*

My subsequent penalty was: construction assignment. Actually, it was *de*struction but they called it construction anyway. I'd make little rocks out of big ones for concrete mix. The idea was to keep everybody busy, exhausted and out of trouble.

First morning at 6:00 am after breakfast in Mess Hall, I now had the work "privilege" of hopping into the back of a pickup truck with five other inmates. We were taken to a distant area to piles of rocks. *No whistling!*

The Hack dumped us with one large and one small pneumatic jack hammer and a generator. Nobody said anything. When the Hack drove off, coffee grounds and metal cups appeared as if from nowhere.

Texas winter is bitter and a torrid cup of coffee could light you up inside and make it bearable. Well, sort of.

A rusty pot appeared out of thin air; a scrounged fire ignited, water boiled. Smuggled coffee grounds tossed, steeped and sank to the bottom. This was magical! Desperate men, resourceful and determined, prevailed.

I weighed 155 pounds. My regulation khakis afforded little warmth. I shivered and glanced around wide-eyed.

The Seagoville compound seemed vast. Activities ranged from knocking down to building up or renovating various make-work projects.

We might be left to ourselves beside a Quonset hut with the order to rotate 200 bags of cement. Or, the day's work might consist of digging a ditch for a driveway.

At lunch time the pickup returned. We piled in back and were driven to Mess Hall, Building 8. Every inmate queued up with a lunch tray and walked the cafeteria line. Institution food was fresh and plentiful and hot.

Our food had been grown on site at the Seagoville farm. It was tasty but often infiltrated with an errant insect corpse: green bugs with spinach. Sometimes, there were yellow bugs with squash, or was it squashed bugs with yellow? If you're famished, what difference could it make? We were always hungry after work.

Fresh cold milk contained the cream, so there was nothing to complain about. Nobody listened anyway. No one talked. We shared the same reality of monotony and the monotony of reality itself.

Four line counts occurred each day without fail; before work, at lunchtime, after supper and at lockdown for sleep at 9:00 pm. Mail call came at 6:00 pm.

To receive a letter was problematic. It was Catch-22 regulations at work. A letter would not be delivered unless the sender was on your approved list, but, how would you know ahead of time who was going to write?

If your list was full you had to remove an old name to receive a letter from a new person. Institutions make rules—not for efficiency—for control.

The thrill when a letter arrived and your name was called cannot be explained, understood or felt by anybody unless they've been in lock up. It is the center of all human happiness. The psychologies of prison were a push and pull at the same time. Each day was a tightrope walk with unknown harms looming below.

*****

After Mess Hall we snapped to the line count. Line count never varied. At least we hoped for a quick one. Otherwise, we were stuck standing and standing.

The Hack walked the line and counted by two's. He phoned the Control Room and waited for a confirmation ring. If the count didn't match, another count was immediate. If the second count did not match—all the buildings went into "lockdown." Every month an escape was attempted and every month they were caught.

The *habituated* man with a free place to live and good food seldom wanted to be set loose at a minimum wage job in the free world. Parole led to a worse kind of prison.

The decision to run off and get captured seemed a no-brainer. It seemed so counter-intuitive that a man just offered parole would commit and act so self-destructive! Escape added five years. These men were called *institutionalized*. Freedom was not the cure.

"We grow too soon old and too late smart," my grandfather use to recite.

*****

Jehovah's Witnesses had a network of communication established. Some of the Brothers had jobs in the Administration Building and knew within minutes when a new JW had arrived. Word got out.

It was a huge relief to know you had allies in sufficient numbers to necessitate two separate congregations.

I became familiar with a wide variety of personalities and we formed a "family."

The *Band of Brothers* is a coalition formed wherever men are thrown together under conditions of tense duress. Prison was transformative. What a peculiar way to finally discover how to be a part of something with impenetrable solidarity. I quickly made close friendships with some fellows who had incredible personalities and intellects. Among them were Joe Pruitt, Ron Clayton, Tollie Padgett, Sammy Salamy, Danny Beene, Richard Bunch and Buddy Thompson.

The married Brothers had a more difficult time of it. The anxiety and sense of loss away from family intensified the pressure of daily living. By contrast, I, the young virgin boy, had no such mental obstacle to face.

I was introduced to a more profound awareness of the doctrines of my religion when I joined Brother Padgett's Bible Study group. We discussed the early years of the Watch Tower Society. Padgett used the Socratic Method. He would ask questions about *your* questions to get you to think about what you thought you knew. The epiphany soon followed! I *thought* I knew and I didn't know at all. An entirely different layer of foundation existed beneath the structure of Witness theology and doctrine. The same was becoming true of me, as well.

A rhythm to life set in with the regularity of a grandfather clock. There was a *tick* and you knew exactly when and where the *tock* would come. I came to rely on procedure, routine, conditioning and group thinking. I was drone in a hive of worker bees.

All my life I had been alone and a loner. I couldn't interface easily. Odd-man-out. Jehovah's Witnesses are self-styled oddballs and misfits. By the process of becoming the *same* we absorbed each other's strengths and banished weakness.

Reminds me of an old Twilight Zone episode with the woman who is the ugliest person in the world who must be operated on to make her conform in looks to her society. The entire drama is photographed with concealing shadows and odd angles. Mysterious!

When the bandages are removed the doctors and nurses cringe in horror—the plastic surgery has failed!

The twist-ending brings the reveal: she is actually beautiful and the rest of her world is hideous. *My bandages* remained in place, so to speak.

I set myself the task of reading and memorizing things in detail. With all this time on my hands; why shouldn't I? For instance, I committed to memory about 850 scriptures. This was hubris, naturally.

Yet, I was eager to transcend the sense of being "average" rank and file. If I could excel at what was expected of me there would be more to my sense of worth than going along to get along. I could be on my way to a status of greater respect by my fellows. I wanted to be *special* and indispensable. I had talents ready to kick in and expand.

Inside the Federal Prison I viewed the microcosm of personality, behavior and self-expression as a kind of laboratory of humanity under pressure.

These men, each in his own way, were coming to terms with a life at odds with his own desire and preferences.

Coping with frustration threw them on either their best talents or their worst resourcefulness. Naturally, no man who is a criminal is inclined to honest stratagem or tactics.

The range of insidious talent for getting what they wanted was mind-boggling for its variety of dodges and camouflage. Criminals are natural actors playing their role of victim, The goal is misdirection and opportunism.

For a criminal to take advantage of your weaknesses they must first disarm you as to their intentions and propensity for predatory malevolence. Survival of the fittest. *I was about to achieve failure.*

Your closest family members might arrive for visit. Hugs, smiles, then an awful silence after the first few minutes of greeting inevitably followed. A stunning absence of mutual context is a real conversation killer.

This was excruciating to crave contact with family and friends only to end up groping for anything to say.

The news carried in would stab you in the heart because you suddenly remembered the life you no longer lived. Visits were a sweet misery.

You could not live without them but, they messed you up mentally for days on end. Married men had it the worst, no doubt about that.

To access the visiting room all the inmates had to strip stark naked. We awkwardly faced away from the Hack. Then, as unthinkable as it may seem to you sitting there in your civilized world, we were forced to bend forward and grab the cheeks of our butt and spread them so the lucky guard could walk by and peer into our bowels for god-knows-what smuggled contraband!

Sure, what visitor wouldn't look forward to such a gift? I pray no guard ever really took the trouble to look.

After the visit was over it was worse. If a wife or girlfriend happened to visit, you could only kiss and embrace once upon arrival and once before the end of your visit.

Men who have not even looked at a real woman for months on end have a predictable reaction to being able to embrace and kiss one. Mae West said it best, "Are you glad to see me or is that a gun in your pocket?" I can assure you it was not a gun.

Back in the strip-down all the erections that wouldn't go away saluted the Hack who now had to contend with rude penises and gaping rectums. It takes a special kind of person to take on a job like that!

Those of us who were innocent Jehovah's Witness boys did not find it amusing or natural. We found it humiliating and degrading and excruciating to experience the betrayal of our body to forces beyond prayer or self-control.

Now, with the passage of time, I can see how prudish and cloistered we were and how funny it is we were impractical and squeamish as all that.

I can't imagine what the sweet Sister from the Kingdom Hall must have been thinking when all these fine Christian Brothers stood up to leave with a baseball bat in their pants!

You can make anything nasty in your own mind if you are taught to do so. Unfortunately, that is exactly what we learned from our Watchtower studies.

In the real world young men can relieve themselves with masturbation. Jehovah's Witnesses don't live in *that* world. They aren't allowed. So, the pressure of such guilt mixed with mental and physical urges was simply unnecessarily worse. Straw—meet camel's back.

A rational person would look at what we were and what was required of us and wonder why our own religion seemed out of touch with compassion. Where was the humanity? Isn't Christianity about forgiveness?

What non-Jehovah's Witnesses cannot understand is this: JW's are not under "grace" the way mainstream Christianity identifies believers as simply *forgiven* for their human nature and everyday failings. We had to earn our forgiveness moment to moment under a probationary—"What have you done for me lately?"

Additionally, we weren't certain where we stood with the inmate population either. Who and what was dangerous? One false step with God or man was ever on our collective mind.

New J-Dubs in Seagoville had to discover everything worth knowing the hard way. The *hard way* was to listen and learn by context, observation and a kind of sixth sense. If you didn't catch on quickly enough it could be dangerous for you.

Theoretically, I was safe in a "minimum" security prison. This was a theory about to be tested and what would be disconfirmed was unimaginable.

The real world was a wrecking ball.

Prison was a closed system.

Conservation of Evil was the Law.

*****

1967-1969 SEAGOVILLE
NEMESIS

Detention buildings crowded in like bullies taunting small children. Another inmate was trying to say something to me. He's my best friend. His voice snapped me back. I fought my way into the present tense.

Danny Beene's voice was slowly reaching me. He was forcing me to focus. He had befriended me recently.

I stood shaking as though a cold wind had blown through my soul.

"He had me and I couldn't move! In that warehouse back there...that storage building..."

"Who did what?" Danny, a JW like me, encouraged and uplifted every one of us every way he could.

"Hajim; he's the guy who always wears those mirror-sunglasses. You've seen him." I may as well have been a robot at that moment. I answered mechanically.

"He hurt you?" I could see the gathering concern in Danny's face. I would not or *could not* focus on what happened. (Not yet.)

Earlier that day, an inmate fell in beside me as I made my way out of building 4.

He wore a Muslim cap and mirrored shades like Thelonious Monk. Something was on his mind.

Hajim dogged my steps in order to say something.

He was a hulking figure I often observed on his down-time in the Weight Shack beside the pond. Inevitably, he'd be furiously pumping iron.

Inmates don't go out of their way to talk with Jehovah's Witnesses. This guy was mumbling something about his wife and a Bible study. None of it was clear. I guessed he had some question. It didn't strike me as provocative.

He was reaching out for some reason. None of what he said had clear context. Too much time away from women turned men only two ways eventually: weak or desperate. Apparently Hajim needed to cross that line.

I pieced together he was heading off to change out fluorescent bulbs in a warehouse. I was asked to go with him while he talked.

He worked on the electrician crew on assigned duty.

"I got me some questions about Bible sayings. You explain it to me. You understand?"

That was all he said and wheeled around, heading off for a squat, grey building secluded from the main compound.

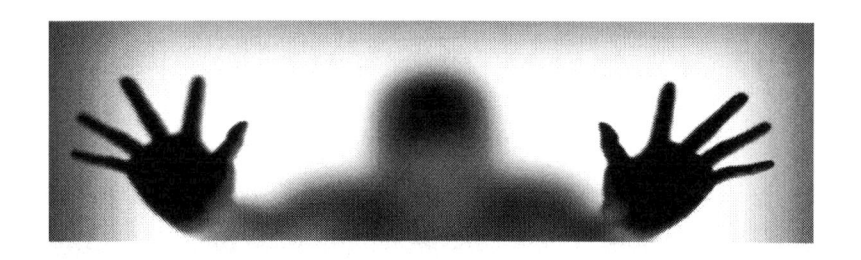

THE BELLY OF THE BEAST

I shrugged and marched behind Hajim with time to spare. An hour lay fallow before me like an empty field before a plow. It was so natural a thing to do. I was obligated and duty called.

Jehovah's Witnesses, even in prison, had to preach when the opportunity arose. Hajim knew this too. There were only wolves and sheep in this world.

Today, Hajim comes as a sheep. The *real* sheep follows ever so meekly.

Up the stairs into a breeze way, we two figures plodded forward with footfalls echoing as the rattle of bones.

The day inched into greyness toward darkness.

Shadows gulped and swallowed us into the building's hulking gut.

The dark, rectangular man with his shades and thin moustache pushed open a sturdy door and stepped aside inviting me to precede him.

The vastness of the room sprawled inward into outlines unseen and disturbingly monstrous.

There are only two important moments: before and afterward. In between hangs *the moment.*

One moment the world hangs balanced in space; the next, everything comes unstuck as a passage from life to humiliation.

It happened with the swiftness of a serpent's strike! The first minute, I blinked to adjust to shadows and black nothingness; the next, I spied the door as it *was being locked.*

Locked? Why? Some trap was sprung on someone too stupid to beware!

This was a consummate betrayal. The brutal urgency of the attack unhinged me to the point I stopped thinking as a human being.

I was fiendishly seized from behind. The audacious, strong-limbed inmate had shrewdly pounced with such uncanny grace, unwitting me! I dangled in the air aloft as a scrawny marionette.

A baffling prodding from behind caught me stupefied.

A crumpled thought twisted into horror: Hajim is humping me like a big dog with its bitch: me!

I squirmed and arched my back to fend away his ruinous assault.

His hot chest and pounding heart drummed against my spine.

A bestial voice exhaled pestilence upon my neck. Low and ruminative pleasure grunts, hound-like, echoed in the room.

"Give me what I want, man or I'll knock you out and take it."

This was not even a threat: this was certainty.

Cold objectivity flooded in upon me. Something inside screamed. Soundless, empty air rushed out of my dry mouth.

A hapless heart flailed, rattling in a cage in my chest.

My assailant's voice barked provocative commands.

"…take you out! Teach you everything…"

Icy clarity seized my consciousness, simple childish thoughts:

Wasn't I a servant of God's will?

Why me? Why this?

Adrenaline is a sordid intoxicant, jumbling my thoughts. . . all senses on high alert, thrusting from behind; this vile dance mocked my sense of God. "You are never tested beyond what you can endure. . ." Jehovah could make the way out!

I spoke as calmly as if I were explaining to a child:

"*I can't do this.* **It is against my religion**."

Bland, calm Statements. . . as though read from the label of a can. Contents: "religious nitwit with dumb commitment and self-destructive determination."

Muscular arms looped under my pits and steel-fingered hands interlaced behind my head. The lifting power of this monster was extreme!

The baffling impropriety was clear. Only God could end this now.

Unconnected thoughts shunted in and out of my head.

Abraham raised the dagger to plunge into his only son's chest! The angel *stayed his hand.*

This was *that* moment...

I had placed myself in the hands of the living God.

The rest was up to Him.

The rest...God *willed.*

Reckoning

There was no clever argument left and no authority to claim otherwise. A "dagger" had plunged.

What excuse was I supposed to make to absolve Jehovah in all this?

I was no martyr or messiah. I was a child in the eyes of the law, not even 21 years old. I was a *lamb*.

After the incident, I was dazed, spaced out and finally dead calm. Nobody knew *Post Traumatic Stress* as a natural consequence of extreme shock in the year 1968. Men were expected to tough it out and never indulge in angst or hand-wringing displays.

I mean, really—what had I expected? This was me alone in the world discovering what was and wasn't reality.

The *wrecking ball* had taken my head off! Disconfirmation of certainty hit me between my eyes.

My first consideration was how this was going to reflect on Jehovah's Witnesses. I was nothing to them but a symbol of the faithful rain dance always ongoing.

If I broke and asked to transfer to Alternate Service in the hospital at this point I'd be marked as a loser whose lack of faith brought on his own ruination. I would let my fellow inmates down and become a laughing stock.

If I bucked up and brushed it off and took the bit between my teeth and charged ahead—well, it was only what was expected of me anyway.

At best, I was somebody who had passed a sadistic minimum requirement *test of faith* and now, if I so chose, would continue in provisional standing.

I relied on prayer and total service to Jehovah until this moment. How had that worked out for me so far?

It hadn't. My ordeal was only what I had done *lately*.

I had no permanent standing with my God or my religion.

Later

"What are you trying to tell me?" Lt. Bennet's voice filled the room.

His office stood pristine with surfaces shining and perfect like the polished mirrored glaze on the lieutenant's shoes.

His motto was: Get to the point or get the hell out!

Impatient and insistent; he listened anyway.

Inmate Tollie Padgett's folder lay open on the desk before him.

Padgett was another JW, one of the inmate leaders of the 40 incarcerated non-combatants and a bit older than the rest, a college graduate.

Padgett had written a "cop-out" form requesting a personal hearing.

Inmate request forms served as the permanent record of inquiry and communication between inmates and staff.

Prison is bureaucracy, especially a federal prison.

Bennet appraised requests, all of them. He was the final arbiter, the court of final inquiry and the warden's prime minister.

Padgett was bid to sit down in a chair the color of despair.

"One of the Brothers was attacked by another inmate. . ."

"Which inmates are we talking about here?"

(It is never safe to snitch names; there is an unwritten code of zero tolerance.)

Officers asked anyway to see how each man negotiated, persuaded, lied or begged. This was an x-ray for character and honesty.

"Inmate Terry Walstrom, Y-11857, was the victim and I don't know the name of his attacker. I can tell you which building and what room the perpetrator is in, though."

Bennett leaned forward instinctively as though a thought had crossed his mind.

"Exactly what went down and why isn't your 'Brother' in here telling me himself if he is an injured party?"

Padgett pursed his lips and glanced thoughtfully to the side.

"He's—I guess, not talking—at least, not in any detail. He doesn't exactly know what to do. The perpetrator pretended to be interested in hearing about what we Jehovah's Witnesses believe. He used that to lure Brother Walstrom into one of those storage warehouses behind Mess Hall. He grabbed him from behind and threatened him."

"Threatened what?"

This sort of incident was more uncommon than people on the outside would ever believe.

Inmates could find anything they want inside the fence. It isn't necessary to use force. Something was awry. Prisoners quickly learned how to barter and negotiate. The price, if right, brought everything but freedom.

"My guess—this other inmate wanted to force sex on Brother Walstrom. This happened yesterday around this time."

Bennett grinned sardonically and shifted back in his chair. He turned toward the window and looked out across the compound. It was noon, or, a little past.

Inmates were scurrying around like toy soldiers on patrol. Bennett put his arms behind his head and clasped his hands for thoughtful support.

"You guess? You either know something or you don't. Why are you wasting my time?"

Padgett could sense he was about to be tossed out. This was the time to get right to the point.

"I know this Brother; I know his temperament and character."

"Something terrible happened. He isn't talking because he doesn't know how to deal with what happened. He is very likely ashamed and filled with rage. I would be!"

Bennett listened dispassionately. JW's were boys among men.

What did they expect?

"Well, now, when he is ready to tell me what did or didn't occur, I'll be all ears."

Bennett threw a meaningful glance Padgett's way. It was a dismissal.

Rising anger took hold as Padgett walked toward the office exit. He pivoted and faced Bennett.

"Sir, if the Brothers are being molested it is *your* responsibility to investigate!"

Bennett flinched imperceptibly. His face suffused with blood.

Then, he gained icy control and made not a move or a sound. That was his own tactic and he wouldn't rise to bait.

"Really? You boys aren't Bennett's Witnesses are you? What the hell does Jehovah do all day?"

Padgett stared briefly, then exited. He and the other guys would take care of it.

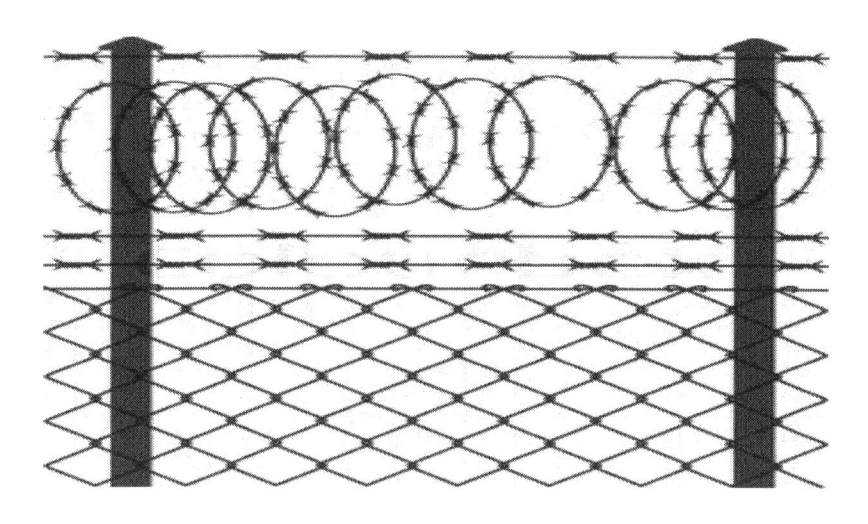

CAPACITY FOR VIOLENCE

Years later, somebody asked me a question which had a very simple answer. The answer was so simple it had to be laughed off as ridiculous.

"Why would a person who had trained in karate refuse to use it if they had been attacked?" The answer is this: In a real life situation you suddenly discover for the first time whether or not you have the *capacity for violence.* Without that inherent, core identity—all the training in the world becomes reduced to a less than meaningless abstract. Practice sessions aren't REAL!

You may want to hurt somebody very badly and even have good reason. Surprisingly, you are either made that way or you are not. There is no middle ground.

How surprised I turned out to be!

You think you know what you would have done, but, really—do you know? Besides, how much scorn would attach to a conscientious objector who used karate on another inmate? There was no win possible.

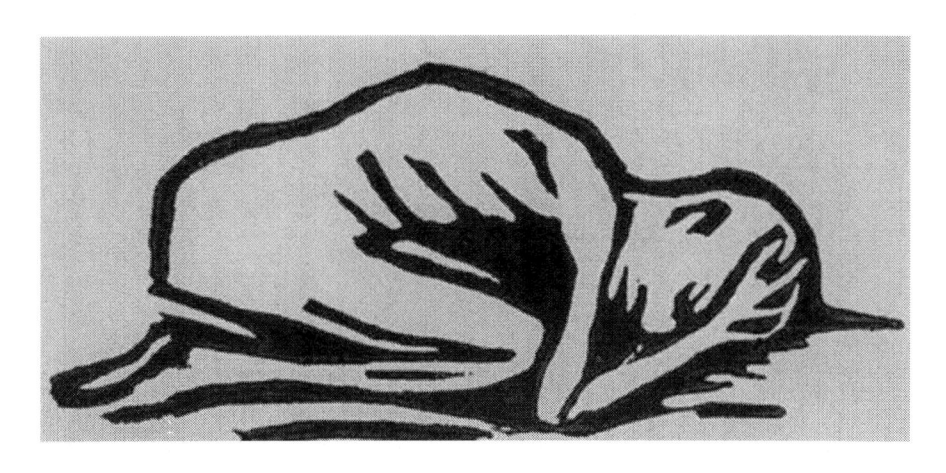

Aftermath

I couldn't sleep. I had revenge fantasies. Daily I plotted tripping "accidentally" with boiling coffee in my hand as I passed Hajim's seat in the Mess Hall.

I kept a two-by-four under my bed at night. I suffered the first of many ongoing panic attacks. Mostly I was sad beyond tears. I felt as though somebody I dearly loved had suddenly died.

But no—it was only innocence.

*****

Final Argument to the Jury

What was lost and what was gained? What I had lost was gone and something ugly remained in its place.

I pushed it down like a powerful spring until it locked inside. I turned my mind inward and twisted hell into a kind of sunshine of denial; denial erased everything. Life was *improvisation as a*nother year passed.

I sought normal life. I wanted family. I blended.

Parole granted, I returned to my local Kingdom Hall. The Congregation's Presiding Overseer actually met me at the door with a sign-up form in his hand. He wanted me to jump into full-time ministry! Where was *Hello*?

I signed up for door-to-door "Pioneering," one hundred hours a month. I gave it all I had until I had no more to give. My rain dance was sputtering to a dry halt.

I should have written this book 44 years ago, yet I could not do it. I had pushed it all the way down too far to retrieve. Frankly, the idea of how all this would read held me back as well. Who wants to spit into the wind and have your life fly back into your face?

Nothing can replace the high of being absolutely certain. It is the ultimate drug. *I'm right and you're wrong.* This thinking makes you who you think you deserve to be.

There was a God-shaped hole in the center of life. It was a phantom limb on an amputee. I'd say to my true self, "It is better than having that foot on my neck again."

Pontius Pilate asked Christ "What is "Truth?"

I can just see every Jehovah's Witness on the planet right now waving their Watchtower in the air, grinning.

Other men's opinions cannot be our *truth*. We have a conscience for a reason. Faith and belief are the way to *avoid* looking through Galileo's telescope.

Why investigate if you are *already* right? See the pitfall waiting there? Nobody needs to test what they "know."

Are you dancing for rain until you drop on dry ground?

I was. What happens when total certainty is disproved?

Where will you go next? Do you give up on belief, faith and God? Or, do you find refuge in an honest admission we are *ignorant*—but—so is everybody else who claims God is whispering in their ear: *"Hubris!"*

I don't know and neither do you.

With those last few words I close the book, ring the bell and blow out the candle.

"If you want to keep a secret, you must also hide it from yourself."
— George Orwell, 1984—

The Good Samaritan

A story is told in the Bible book of Luke about a despised, apostate Samaritan who is moved by his conscience to help a total stranger injured beside a roadway. Jesus reveals this apostate is qualified for eternal life for loving his neighbor more than the priest who had passed by on the other side *to avoid giving aid*. Imagine that! An apostate *worthier* than an anointed priest!

Hospital Service

I motored over to Dub's house. It is early Sunday morning and he's ready to go even though I'm early.

We drove to the rehabilitation hospital.

"Who can volunteer to provide some Spiritual encouragement for the patients on the 3rd floor of Texas Rehabilitation Hospital?", Dub's Bible study group at the Unity Church had been asked by hospital coordinators.

Dub jumped at the chance. "Jumped" is perhaps the wrong word. Dub has a missing leg. At least the original organic part is missing.

A prosthetic device has replaced it. You might call it his "stand in."

Dub used to be a Baptist preacher. In fact, he studied at 3 seminaries. Now, he is eighty-five. Involuntarily he "retired" from the ministry after a car crash crushed his leg and dislodged his left eye. That was in 2003. It was a life changer for him!

His world and worldview, he had confided, turned upside down over night. He was no longer "viable" as a Pastor. This was his Church's verdict. Inevitably, he was unplugged from active relevance in not only the church but his family as well. His eyes were opened to unpleasant awareness. Life was going to be very different!

Dub Horn began questioning things. He set aside his rigid mindset. His new self accepted the freedom of new opportunity. A chance to be of some service to others doesn't come often (if at all) for a man in his 80's.

He was eager to take on the special job of visitation and morale booster for the third floor at the rehab ward. If ever a man was well-suited for such a task it was Dub.

That's where I came in.

Although I had never before volunteered for charity work, I thought it was time I left my comfort zone and offered "mankind" some payback. It was time to care about others.

Dub was a regular customer of mine at the bookstore where I worked: Half-Price Books.

For an avid reader such as me it was a dream-come-true.

My job was to sort and shelve books in the Religion and Philosophy sections.

About once or twice a week, Dub would putter up in his motorized wheelchair and meander back to the Religion section searching for a chat.

I could tell right away he was warmly knowledgeable. He also displayed a pleasant "people person" manner. We *clicked*. 'Very cheery man', I thought.

Soon after my retirement, Dub and I met for coffee once a week and we'd catch up. He turned to me one day and said, *"I've got a job for you if you're interested..."*

Something inside me responded positively to the suggestion and I accepted, although I confess, I had never done this sort of thing before. I had no idea what was ahead, but, it isn't too often at my age (mid-sixties) I can indulge a fresh, positive experience.

The third floor of Rehab Hospital is vast. It is dedicated to *special* cases that aren't nominally a perfect fit. As a matter of fact, the people who reside there have little actual hope of rehabilitation. These particular patients have a terminal prognosis.

Dub and I arrived. I parked in the Handicap zone and Dub hung his special sign on my rearview. I unloaded Dub's case and we took the long trek upstairs to the 3rd floor. There I unpacked the speakers for music and organized his clippings and print-outs and connected speaker wires to his iPad.

This particular Sunday morning, after setting up the CD player with soothing Old Time Gospel music (foreign to my virgin ears), I took a seat on the nearby couch. This room for visitors and patients is arranged comfortably with actual home-style furniture.

After a few minutes, one by one, the cavalcade of wheel chairs arrives. Nurses tool them in and position the seating arrangement into a spacious semi-circle.

(Imagine a large den with cushy furniture and nobody seated on anything but their wheelchairs.)

Unexpectedly, I was rather shaken by my first sight of three catatonic patients ferried in and arrayed in the front of the room. Each was elderly, frail and contorted in some physical manner.

I held my breath involuntarily until I finally confronted them as people and realized what their state of being was and how their minds were trapped in unresponsive bodies!

I squirmed inside my own healthy body. (It felt like guilt.) I actually had to remind myself: This isn't about you, Terry, this isn't about you.

The first catatonic person, a middle-aged lady, merely slumped with her head drooped down, with doll's eyes partly closed. The second woman's head permanently tilted as if to examine the ceiling.

One other patient was a stare-straight-ahead lady, inert in a way impossible for me to comprehend.

All the usual possibilities for social interaction did not apply. At least, so it seemed to me. Being cordial or friendly had always seemed to be about manners and conversation, gestures and formality.

None of that meant anything in this situation.

A rude thought intruded: an impression of awkward, discomfiting statues and not people. (This was a living person?)

Immediately, other patients wheeled in by nurses, wedged the interstices in a loose array.

Another white-haired lady who hummed or sang wordlessly without tune caught my attention. She, for an hour and a half, continued the singsong, deeply rooted in her own lodged "memory."

Next to her sat an alert woman actively engaging everybody and nobody in particular. Every sentence commenced with, "I adopted two kids in Nigeria. ... In school they call the boy I adopted 'the rich kid' because I sent him clothes and shoes. ... I have photographs...."

Over and again this person shared her one essential thought with the group, perhaps like a phonograph needle, her brain is stuck in one groove....always.

On her left was a Church of Christ member (so she told us) who responded to everything Dub would say by repeating it exactly as a human echo.

When either of us would say something aloud one particular lady spoke up to say "You're a wonderful man" It never failed to sound perfectly sincere.

This woman appeared as though she had just arrived home from church. Her grooming was perfect and her sweet smile glowed with benevolence.

Before our hour and a half had ended, she had repeated that pet phrase exactly fifteen times. (I know, I counted for some obsessive reason of my own!) "You're a wonderful man. You're a wonderful man."

Each utterance was as though for the very first time.

I had burrowed into myself emotionally at this point. I confess I had become an observer, as though I were in a strange jungle of indescribable flora and fauna.

An outsider in a strange new world, I asked myself, "What next?"

****

The last man in our crowded parlor was a dignified ninety-year old black gentleman who informed us modestly he had been a Deacon in his church for many years.

He confessed he was no longer good at sharing conversationally but could express himself in song. We did not hesitate to encourage him!

He began crooning, "He Touched Me," in a mellow, deep voice that lovingly caressed each phrase. I listened enthralled by the power of his performance.

Dub's face shone moist with tears flowing from his eyes as I suddenly experienced something unaccustomed and unidentifiable inside. An emotion was escaping from the prison of my soul as the Deacon's plaintive song ended on a pianissimo of gentle praise.

Dub choked out, "When I had my head-on collision and lost my leg, I was in the hospital for six months. One day, a pretty young lady came to the hospital and up to my room and sang that same song for me: "He Touched Me". I felt like God wanted me to know he cared about my suffering.. ..."

At this point, I should mention an incessant background sound floating in the air.

It was a woman's plaintive voice repeating a phrase from a distance. Perhaps she was in another room?

It grew louder until her bed appeared at the doorway as the floor nurse wheeled her in and trundled her to the back of the room and locked the brake on the bed's wheels.

We heard her voice so often it became the patter of rain or the sound of wind in an uncomfortable downpour. She called politely but beseechingly!

"Help me, please. Somebody help me. Please help me, somebody."

None of the patients blinked an eye her way. Dub gave me a searching look.

Shortly, I couldn't bear it any longer. I jumped up and went in search of hospital personnel. I caught up with a nurse. She listened to me and then shook her head despairingly. "She does this. She can't help it. We aren't ignoring her. It is just her thing; part of her symptom."

Let me tell you, if you are hearing it for the first time you feel like a monster for not rushing over and trying to do...what? Something. Anything. The awful reality of it is: there is nothing to be done!

One middle-aged fellow who had suffered a stroke sat in his wheelchair. His wife stood behind him constantly patting him on the arms or rubbing his shoulder in perpetual reassurance and consolation.

She was unfailingly encouraging and tender. I recited to myself silently, "In sickness and in health..."

The man's face owned one expression and it never changed: oblivion. He might well have been a drawing of a man.

Dub stood and explained to everybody we were not there to preach to them but to "encourage them."

Dub Horn is very good at this. Let me tell you; what he says and does is outside of my experience as the Jehovah's Witness I once was for 20 years. There had been no such thing as charity for strangers, only fellow members.

You might say we thought our message was charity enough.

Dub's manner is tenderly personal yet neutral as to an agenda. He smiles genuinely and asks simple questions and gives affirmations. He has no reading material to peddle in order to acquire a convert. He is a beacon and there are always troubled ships foundering out there on rough seas. Unglamorous and yet, magnificent…my friend is anonymous, invisible as he speaks.

"We are here today because God wants us to be together to encourage one another. We don't have to get out and go to a big fancy church to do that. We just gather and His Spirit is with us."

There are a few nods and an old fashioned "amen" or two from the Deacon. I am amused.

Dub continues…

"Why are we still here? Why are we living so long with so many discouraging problems in our health? I'll tell you why: God still has something important for each one of us to do with our lives before he calls us home."

I immediately call to mind the line in Rime of the Ancient Mariner: *"He listens as a three years child; the Mariner hath his will."*

Among our tight group are faces which are mostly flesh facades. The patients seem impassive at first, yet... do I see a flicker of change?

(This is not possible, I'm projecting and not seeing anything.*)*

Dub smiled. He was light and conversational. He sat on a tall cushion about 3 feet off the floor at about eye-level to those seated in wheelchairs.

"What does God want with us? What is our purpose now that we can hardly move about any longer? Well, what are we doing today? We are just sitting here, right? Did you know by YOU being here with me you have *encouraged* me? That's what you've done for ME today.

I hope I can do the same for you and tell you: "God knows you and loves you and will never leave you in your time of distress."

What I like about his delivery is that it has no "preacher" in it at all.

He is just a person, a civilian, a fellow sufferer who has spent his last 8 or 9 years struggling against setback after setback. He is real.

The faces of the catatonic listeners reflect...something... again, I can't exactly say what it is.....but, it is definitely a change of character or mood ...or...

I'd compare it to looking out upon a lake and the water is reflecting the movement of the clouds.

Dub continues...

"I'm here to encourage you to love. God is love. He lives in us when *we* love. Some of you cannot move and yet your mind moves. You can hear. You can think. God has your undivided attention you might say."

"Search in your own heart."

"Is there somebody in your life who has wronged you? If you say to yourself '*I hate so-and-so,*' you aren't hurting them one little bit. But, you are hurting yourself."

"Let go of that. Forgive. Feel love instead of hate for that person who wronged you. It won't do anything for them—but I'll tell you truly: it will allow the love of God to shine inside you."

The energy in this visiting room has as a kind of weather change occurring between sunlight and clouds before a rain. I think I am sensing something.

Dub grins and starts to sing: "This Little Light of Mine, I'm gonna let it shine...."

He waves his hands like a maestro before a motionless orchestra as he sings... and slowly...a few voices join him!

As this goes on, more wheel chairs with more patients are pushed into the room. One new lady is profoundly affected by some sort of palsy.

Her head and eyes roll constantly. It is disconcerting to encounter for the first time! One of the other ladies cries aloud: "She's crazy!"

Dub stops singing and calmly holds his hand toward the unkind remark palm down and quietly remonstrates:

"We don't say that...we say...she has different opportunities than the rest of us..."

The offending lady immediately sees wisdom in this.

"Yes. Yes she does. She has different opportunities than the rest of us."

And the singing continues, "Let it shine, let it shine, let it shine."

By the end of our time in that Visiting room, I can feel all sorts of things happening inside of me I file away for thinking about later. Mostly, I reflect on how very little of my life spent as a Jehovah's Witness was an actual outreach to somebody with profound physical needs to gift them with anything simple like companionship or a word of encouragement. It seems my purpose before was more of prospecting for *customers.* (Peculiar thought!)

It shook me and rocked my world on that amazing 3rd floor. So little can really mean so much!

I called to mind a moment when I sat with a Witness friend in a shopping mall food court sipping coffee years earlier. A deaf man approached our table as we were talking.

The man silently offered my companion his card with American Sign Language printed on it. It requested a donation.

My JW friend looked toward him appraisingly and asked slowly: "You can't hear?" He watched the fellow as he articulated his gestured reply.

Then, my JW friend shook his head "No."

He handed the card back. The deaf fellow nodded at him and walked off to another table. The friend turned to me, apparently pleased with himself.

"I watched his eyes as I spoke to see if he was reading my lips or not. If he's really deaf, he will. If not, he's faking." What made me uncomfortable about that at the time? I thought about it today for some reason. Why must we judge the needs of others? Why had I just sat there like a stone?

Dub has experienced a wonderful visitation this amazing Sunday and so have I. I speculated to my cheerful companion making remarks concerning each person we met up on the 3rd floor. Who are they now compared with what they once were? What sort of life was theirs?

I jabber compulsively for a while. Relief is needed. It is as if I have to debrief myself and talk endlessly about our experience to deal with the **feelings** I'm experiencing. One part of me wanted to flee in terror when I first got there and the other part wanted to hug everybody.

Dub sums it all up nicely. "When we give we always get more in return."

Why hadn't I ever felt this way before? I had to ask.

Dub smiles and shakes his head saliently, "It isn't about you."

And then I suddenly see as if for the first time

It is back!

The tickle of original feeling from when I was only five has returned!

The original God who didn't need a name is present in the act of giving, caring.

Perhaps I am like the Samaritan apostate who listens to conscience?

Perhaps I don't have to be the Priest after all.

*****

Finally, I accept the alternative hospital service.

OLD FRIENDS, NO AMENDS

8 years ago an old Jehovah's Witness friend suddenly popped back into my life after an absence of decades. We had plenty to catch up on.

(**JW**: Jehovah's Witness)

JW: Would you rather have gone to Vietnam than to prison?

Me: That wasn't the choice I faced.

JW: Sure it was.

Me: I might know a little more about that subject than you.

JW: *Oka-a-a-y*. Explain that.

Me: I was called into the Kingdom Hall library by the Overseer and his assistant. Once inside, in confidential tones, they told me what they were about to tell me must never be repeated to any authorities. I was to say it was my Christian conscience and NOT the Watch Tower Society who advised me or coached me or counseled me.

JW: I never knew that.

Me: They said I could comply with the law up to a point. At the point alternate service, such as working in a hospital, was offered I must steadfastly refuse.

JW: Because?

Me: They simply said it was a compromise of *neutrality.*

JW: Well, did you know that, if the Judge sentenced you to hospital work, you could accept that?

Me: Let's say you were standing before a judge who ordered you to slap your daughter as hard as possible, as a penalty for some perceived law she had broken, would you comply?

JW: Certainly not!

Me: A Judge has authority but you have conscience. The option to opt-out is always in place!

JW: What are you saying?

Me: To refuse something is an option that never goes away. "I'm sorry, your Honor, I must decline."

JW: I'll have to think about that one.

Me: "Why do you think so many people leave the Society?"

JW: "I know of maybe 50 to 70 people personally who left the organization after 1975. To me, they were only in the religion to save their own butts and didn't love Jehovah at all. "

Me: "We all spent 7 years trying to *save* people from a totally imaginary event. We pumped up the total membership and sold 108 million books worldwide. For the Watch Tower Society it was a *win* although dead wrong about the date and the false "prophecy."

JW: "I don't regard the Society as *prophets.* So, they can't be guilty of being *false* prophets."

Me: "When those speaking in the name of Jehovah foretell things which do not occur, the Bible's test disconfirms it and it is called **false prophecy**."

JW: "Jehovah *corrected* them. They don't set dates any more. Jehovah allowed them to be embarrassed. Don't think God won't hold them personally responsible for any who were stumbled over that failure."

Me: "If God tells you the truth and it comes out a false prophecy—what is wrong with this picture?"

JW: "Jehovah makes sure all mistakes are corrected. No other religion is willing to correct their mistakes."

Me: "Other religions have *fixed* belief systems. Witnesses have shifting beliefs. When they teach a wrong thing they get tons of letters and phone calls indicating disconfirmation until they change it."

JW: "Which Jehovah can be using *to correct* them. "

Me: "The impact on faithful people is a hard one. Spending your life delivering false information is nothing to be proud of. Lots of Brothers and Sisters quit their job to do full-time preaching of that nonsense. "

JW: "Each Christian has to use his intelligence to know better than to follow the silly stuff they're told by the Elders."

Me: "Are you saying the Elders are not bright enough to do the right thing?"

JW: "I hate to say it; but, 99% of all the Elders I know are just plain stupid!

"If the Watch Tower Society ever tries setting a date again I'll be the first to leave. It won't happen. They have learned their lesson. Jehovah corrected them."

Me: "Oh. Stop me before I kill again!"

*****

What conclusion could I draw from our conversation?

JW doesn't allow any two doubts to touch each other for fear, like raindrops on a window, they will coalesce into a stream that will wash the delusion away and he'll be left feeling very betrayed, indeed.

I Wept By The Rivers Of Babylon Part II:

Tracing The History Of Conscience

LEGACY OF CONSTANTINE

Christianity was made legal by a Roman general!

A military victory secured for Christians what three hundred years of prayer had sought. Persecution was outlawed by the State. Early Christians accepted they had been blessed with a new beginning under a peaceful regime bending over backwards to accommodate them. Perhaps, this intervention was God's way of using the State for the establishment of His son's kingdom on Earth!

This was no revolutionary change in attitude and belief so much as it was evolutionary progress toward harmony. Until Constantine, Christians shunned civil and military service as a matter of conscience. They had imagined themselves citizens of a heavenly regime. Surely, Jesus would come quickly and end all secular human governments, or so they assumed for centuries.

EARLY CHURCH FATHERS

As time passed from the first century to the fourth, we can demonstrate the scruples of Christians toward the Sate. Then, when the 4th Century arrives, a change!

> JUSTIN MARTYR (150 A.D.) "We, who had been filled with war and mutual slaughter and every wickedness, have each one—all the world over—changed the instruments of war, the swords into plows and the spears into farming implements and we cultivate piety, righteousness, love for men, faith, (and) the hope which is from Father Himself through the Crucified One."

> ORIGENES (240 A.D.) "To those who ask us whence we have come or whom we have (for) a leader, we say that we have come in accordance with the counsels of Jesus to cut down our warlike and arrogant swords of argument into plowshares and we convert into sickles the spears we formerly used in fighting.

For we no longer take 'sword against a nation,' nor do we learn any more to make war, having become sons of peace for the sake of Jesus, who is our leader, instead of (following) the ancestral (customs)."

LACTANTIUS (300 A.D.) "For, in the first place, the connection of human society is taken away; for justice cannot bear the cutting asunder of the human race and wherever arms glitter, she must be put to flight and banished. . . . For how can he be just, who injures, hates, despoils, kills?"[7]

CADOUX: "Then too, the conscientious refusal of the Christians to pay divine honors to the emperor and his statue and to take part in any idolatrous ceremonies at public festivities, their aversion to the imperial military service, their disregard for politics and depreciation of all civil and temporal affairs as compared with the spiritual and eternal interests of man, their close Brotherly union and frequent meetings, drew upon them the suspicion of hostility to the Caesars and the Roman people and the unpardonable crime of conspiracy against the State."[8]

---

[7] *Divinae Institutiones* VI vi. pp. 19, 22, by Lactantius, cited in *The Early Christian Attitude to War*, Part II, p. 56 by C. John Cadoux

[8] *Early Church and the World*, p. 189-190, 275-276

Change of Attitude

The changeover from outcast minority to empowered political activists rallied the faith into a change of attitudes.

> "It is generally thought that upon the accession of Constantine to power, the Church as a whole definitely gave up her anti-military leanings, abandoned all her scruples, finally adopted the imperial point of view and treated the ethical problem involved as a closed question. Allowing for a little exaggeration, this is broadly speaking true. The sign of the cross, to which Jesus had been led by his refusal to sanction or to lead a patriotic war and on which he died for the salvation of men, was now an imperial emblem, bringing good fortune and victory. The supposed nails of the cross, which the Emperor's mother found and sent to him, he had made into bridle-bits and a helmet, which he used in his military expeditions."[9]

---

[9] Cadoux: *The Early Church and the World*, pp. 588-589

Paradigm Shift

At this point, in the history of Christian thought, a paradigm shift was about to occur. For three centuries the return of Jesus was expected "shortly." The phrase, "*Come quickly*, Lord Jesus" sums it up succinctly. Even the dullest observer was bound to notice that the passing of three hundred years was a distortion of a reasonable definition of "shortly." Pragmatic men cannot stand around waiting to be rescued forever! Alternate and new expectations replaced old ones.

Instead of passive waiting around for Jesus to do the dirty work in restoring God's will on Earth—4th century Christians would take it upon themselves to create a heaven on Earth through administration of civil government and military solutions: Theocracy.

Within two hundred years, after the so-called Fall of Rome as a world power, the Catholic Church promoted its own ascendance over secular earthly rulers.

In time, the Church was itself a de facto governmental authority; a kind of theologizing of secular power and a secularization of episcopal power.

This Governing Body demanded loyalty by representing itself as the only true mouthpiece of God. Whatever was spoken was true and incumbent. In time, absolute power corrupted the Church making the criticism and accusations of Martin Luther, an apostate monk, impossible to resist. The Reformation was begun.

Eventually, Christianity broke into Protestant and Catholic versions of the Kingdom of God on Earth. Or, to frame the situation in Biblical terms: wheat and weeds.

Who was the wheat? Who were the weeds?

The Catholic Church claimed *magisterium* of tradition and Apostolic succession with infallibility on matters of faith and morals.

Protestantism succumbed to Luther's notion of *sola scriptura*: the Bible alone; every man for himself as aided by Holy Spirit! Absolute certainty was the prize.

When the Church is the same as the State, what possible clash can a man of conscience suffer?

Now that Church and State had separated, personal conscience emerged as guide by necessity. The tension between Church and State was again about to erupt.

Where did this civil war among Christians leave the conscience of Christianity? What about the inevitability of war? What was the individual Christian to do if faced with a *kill or be killed* decision?

The modern concept of a personal Christian conscience became necessary for Protestants; not Catholics.

Augustine's **Just War Theory** provided the necessary foundation for avoiding conflicts in conscience.

What is the Just War?

Augustine asked Christian readers to consider one man hitting a boy and another man caressing a boy. The first man appears to be brutish and evil and yet he might be a father lovingly disciplining his son! The second man appears to be a good and affectionate person, but in fact may well be a child molester! Augustine reasons, "We find a man by love made to appear fierce; and the other man by evil made to appear winningly gentle." This opens the door for Christians to perform outward acts that might appear to be forbidden by Scripture and yet by those acts do a greater good.

Because God judges the soul, the ultimate consideration is not "what the man does ... but with what mind and will he does it." The appropriate motive in all cases, Augustine rules, is love. What is done from love of God must be good. A Christian soldier is under compulsion and love without scruple.

This doctrine was absorbed into the Church and approved as the proper Christian rationale. In his book, *The City of God*, Augustine elucidates his theory. There Augustine insists there is no "private right" to kill. One can kill only under the authority of God, as communicated by direct or implicit command from God, or by a legitimate ruler who carries out God's intent to restrain evil on earth.

Augustine further suggests one who obeys such a command "does not himself do the killing." He acts only as an *instrument of the one who rightfully commands*, without debate.

Augustine concludes, "The commandment forbidding killing was not broken by those who have waged wars under authorization of God, or those who have imposed the death-penalty on criminals when representing the authority of the State, the most just and most reasonable source of power."

When there is no command by God, war may be waged only by those with legitimate authority and only for a just cause. The devil was in that particular detail, however! The Church could declare and it would be so.

As long as the Catholic Church remained both religion *and* State for Christians, the conscience of Christianity remained in repose. Just as God had allowed a transition from Jew to Gentile, He was allowing a transition from pacifism to participation in Civic Authority which included the military.

CONSCIENCE ARISES

Protestant apostasy created a gaping foundational error which cracked open the consciences of non-Catholic Christian worshippers. All the old worries, scruples and conflicts flew out like bats at dusk from a dark cave. If the Church had no actual God-approved authority to declare Just War—on what basis could the Protestant engage in military action? Now was born a new era of conscience. Protestants fell into an every-man-for-himself, case by case, crisis of conscience. The test was often a life or death decision.

"The wars of Israel were the only 'holy wars' in history... there can be no more wars of faith. The only way to overcome our enemy is by loving him."[10]

"All war must be just the killing of strangers against whom you feel no personal animosity; strangers whom, in other circumstances, you would help if you found them in trouble and who would help you if you needed it."[11]

---

[10] *The Cost of Discipleship,* Dietrich Bonheoffer
[11] *The Private History of the Campaign That Failed,* Mark Twain

Modern Pacifism

Pilgrims arrived at Plymouth Rock in the year of our Lord 1620. Within the short space of thirty-six years they were joined by *Mennonites, Amish* and *Hutterites*.

By 1719 the smaller sects were swarming onto the new continent searching for room to practice their unconventional faiths.

Among these were *Dunkers, Shakers, Christadelphians* and *Rogerenes*.

Held in common by these otherwise disparate groups was the assertive audacity to self-identify as pacifists in time of war. This included outright refusal to participate in the defense of hearth and home in Indian uprisings or the Revolutionary War.

The problem with this Bible-based scruple was it was suicidal in practice should everybody suddenly decide to turn the other cheek during a battle. It would only be possible if a majority of Christians took up arms against common foe while the pacifists stood idly by praying!

Contrary Argument

> "The only real objection which can be argued against the revival of the early Christian attitude is that Christianity has accepted the State and that this carried with it the necessity for coercive discipline within and the waging of war without; in which disagreeable duties Christians must as citizens take their part."

"To refuse this will expose civilization to disaster...The truth is that the way of war, if persisted in, is going to destroy civilization anyhow and the continual demand for war service will, sooner or later, bring modern State anarchy ..."

"It is a subject that will not cease to vex the Church until we have decided either to make as unequivocal a condemnation of war as we have of slavery, or to abandon altogether any profession of whole-hearted allegiance to the Christian faith."[12]

---

[12] Cadoux: *Early Christian Attitude to War*, Foreword, p. ix-x, Rev. W.E. Orchard

A DECLARATION

Of the SAD and GREAT
Persecution and Martyrdom

Of the People of God, called
QUAKERS, in *NEW-ENGLAND*,
for the Worshipping of God.

Whereof
- 22 have been Banished upon pain of Death.
- 03 have been MARTYRED.
- 03 have had their Right-Ears cut.
- 01 have been burned in the Hand with the letter H.
- 31 Persons have received 650 Stripes.
- 01 was beat while his Body was like a jelly.
- Several were beat with Pitched Ropes.
- Five Appeals made to *England*, were denied by the Rulers of *Boston*.
- One thousand forty four pounds worth of Goods hath been taken from them (being poor men) for meeting together in the fear of the Lord, and for keeping the Commands of Christ.
- One now lyeth in Iron-fetters, condemned to dye.

ALSO

Some CONSIDERATIONS, presented to the KING, which is in *Answer* to a Petition and Address, which was presented unto Him by the General Court at *Boston*: Subscribed by *J. Endicot*, the chief Persecutor there; thinking thereby to cover themselves from the Blood of the Innocent.

Gal. 4. 29. *But as then, he that was born after the flesh, persecuted him that was born after the Spirit, even so it is now.*

God hath no respect to *Cains Sacrifice*, that killed his Brother about Religion.

London, Printed for *Robert Wilson*, in *Martins Le Grand*.

CONSCRIPTION MEETS CONSCIENCE

Quakers refused the oath of allegiance to the King and sought to create their own theocracy in Pennsylvania.

As if Quakers weren't annoying already, they further staunchly dug in and refused to pay taxes! They reasoned tax money was supporting the war effort. (Revolutionary War, 1775-1783).

Revolutionary authority imprisoned conscientious objectors and seized over one hundred thousand pounds of their personal goods and property as penalty.

These summary confiscations became commonplace. Counterbalancing this sectarian heretical stance was the fact these pious believers were also hard-working, honest to a fault and dependable good neighbors who fulfilled *all other* civic duties.

Mennonites believed God did not condone killing or the use of force for any reason and were therefore unwilling to fight for their lives. They paid especially high taxes for military exemption. Among them were the Amish as an ethnic religious offshoot.

Among German sects were non-conformists; both non-political and less educated.

Mennonites and *Dunkards*, named for their practice of triple dipping baptism, were mostly poor farmers often called upon to supply the army with wagons and horses.

Moreover, what was the alternative but official confiscation? German religious groups complied with confiscation and contributed food, timber, blankets and clothing to keep the troops warm in winter, although they would never agree to participate in any battle.

The first national effort at conscripting young men for war came in March 1863 after two years of Civil War. Congress made it legal for any conscript to find a substitute combatant or pay a fine of $300 to commute his obligation. ($5,555 today.)

*****

In pre-modern instances, use of the term *conscientious objector* is an anachronism. This is for the simple reason it was coined in the late nineteenth century and first found in the Oxford English Dictionary in 1899.

In *Freedom from War: Nonsectarian Pacifism, 1814-1914*, author Peter Brock traced the term "conscientious objection" to military service or war to the year 1846, when it was mentioned several times by pacifists, antimilitarists and political radicals in their campaign against compulsory militia service and recruitment for the British Army.[13]

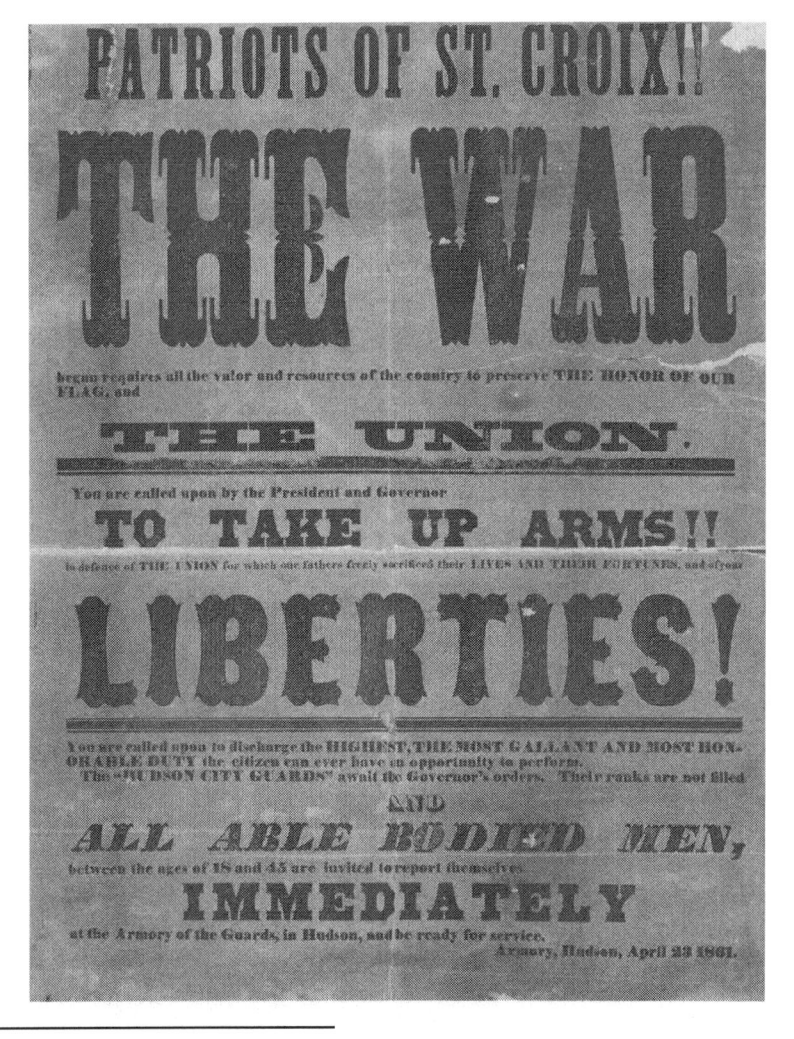

---

[13] *Conscience and Conscientious Objections* Anders Schinkel Amsterdam University Press, Jan 1, 2007

130

The Northern States under federal law amended previous provisions so as to recognize only those conscientious objectors who were members of religious denominations whose rules and articles of faith prohibited armed service.

Place yourself in the position of the townsfolk who are trying to be fair and tolerant. What options were plausible in addressing the social problems at hand? Time and again local citizens made a civilized effort first and then became frustrated, angry and finally violent.

In the Confederacy, the draft law of 1862 exempted *Quakers, Mennonites, Brethren* and *Nazarenes*, with the understanding they would either hire a substitute or pay $500. ($11,627 today)

These conditions were clearly unsatisfactory and many pacifists could either not meet the monetary demand or would refuse hire of someone who might kill in their stead. The conscientious objector often found himself moved to camps in states where no one knew of him or his good reputation. He would be in the hands of military officers who had little or no sympathy for his scruples.

There are records of pacifists who were tortured, hanged by their thumbs or pierced by bayonets for refusing to carry a musket; many others were imprisoned. Some pacifists joined the army as cooks and/or would shoot over the heads of the enemy rather than kill them.[14]

---

[14] *Conscience in America: A Documentary History of Conscientious Objection in America, 1757-1967*, p. 15-26. ed. by Lillian Schlissel

Conscientious objectors in World War I found themselves shipped off to army camps. It was up to them to convince unsympathetic officers and other officials of their sincerity.

Occasionally, the objectors were removed to prisons instead of camps. One source states 3,989 men identified their conscientious objector status when they had reached the camps. Among them, 450 were court-martialed and sent to prison; 940 languished in camps until the Armistice was fully enacted.

The absolutist objector who refused to drill or do any noncombatant service received court-martial and sentences of many years in Federal prison at Alcatraz Island or Fort Leavenworth. Within U.S. Disciplinary Barracks, many suffered persecution, shackling and solitary confinement.[15]

---

[15] *The Politics of Conscience: The Historic Peace Churches and America at War, 1917-1955*, pp. 19-26, 144-146, by Albert N. Keim and Grant M. Stoltzfus (Herald Press, Scottdale, PA, 1988)

Concerned citizens inside and outside of government braced themselves for a radical re-think for workable policies regarding religious persons of conscience; this was called one-W in July of 1952. Provisions offered Civilian Public Service as an alternative to combat that included farming, welfare work, construction and low-level health facility employment.

The positive outcome of providing alternate programs was introducing Mennonite and Brethren to educational careers and participation in social service jobs which included meaningful ways of helping others in their communities. In the early 1950's ten thousand of the one-W men were processed and less than 30 left without authorization. Jehovah's Witnesses comprised 20 of those with negative participation.

VIETNAM WAR 1959-1975

The Vietnam War produced draft resisters working within organized networks. Rejection of conscription stemmed from disagreement with the United States' foreign policy in Indochina. Political activists pointed to perceived injustice against African Americans, the poor and the uneducated.

Civil rights groups and women's organizations soon jumped in and staged massive anti-war rallies in which hundreds of young men burned their draft cards. As a new interpretation, in 1965 the Supreme Court ruled conscientious objectors (or C.O.'s) need not believe in a Supreme Being. This was expanded in 1970 to include individuals objecting to military service on ethical grounds if "deeply felt."

Statistics reveal the breakdown among deferments as follows: Total deferments comprised 170,000 conscientious objectors with 300,000 denied. Total evaders numbered 600,000 with 200,000 formally accused. Canadian draft evaders numbered around 50,000 and another 20,000 either fled to other countries or lived "underground" in the United States.

President Nixon opined ending the draft would end the massive opposition to war, but in this he erred. A pretentious and hollow victory was finally declared and troops abandoned the battle.

> "On September 16, 1974, President Gerald R. Ford issued a proclamation that offered amnesty to those who evaded the draft during the Vietnam War. Mr. Ford also granted amnesty to those in the military who deserted their duty while serving. However, the amnesty came with certain conditions, namely that those involved agreed to reaffirm their allegiance to the United States and serve two years working in a public service job."[16]

---

[16] *The Strength Not to Fight: An Oral History of Conscientious Objectors of the Vietnam War*, pp 6-7, by James W. Tollefson (Little, Brown & Company, Boston, MA, 1993),

*****

BRITONS

"WANTS" YOU

JOIN YOUR COUNTRY'S ARMY!
GOD SAVE THE KING

DENOMINATIONS GRAPPLE WITH WAR

Nine million men in uniform and legions of civilians were slaughtered on the battlefields, battleships and trenches of no-man's-land throughout World War I. Another twenty-one million were permanently scarred and disfigured. Germany's lethal submarine attacks, mustard gas mass killings and aerial bombings created the catalyst for deadlier conflict in WWII. Since the majority of participating nations were predominately Christian, what official position could the various denominations take in view of Christ's admonition to "love your enemy?"

Mormons

In WWI the Mormon Church had only a few hundred thousand members, yet fifteen thousand of their men enlisted in the U.S. Army. Indeed, Mormons were anxious to demonstrate loyalty and affinity with America because of suspicions about them and their teachings.

Church campaigns to enlist Latter Day Saints (LDS) in military ranks as well as conducting Liberty Bond drives established their bona fides. The Mormon Church's leaders held definite positions toward the war, some of which were modified over time.[17]

Catholics

Leftist liberal pacifists refused to register for the draft and rallied support for workers to refuse to work in factories making weapons. Communist Dorothy Day urged American Catholics not to join in the European theater of war. Pope Benedict XV, in his first encyclical immediately following the end of the war, declared:

> "The conscience of Christianity had been scarred by its own advocates."

> "The blame certainly must be laid on ministers of the Gospel."[18]

---

[17] *Mormonism in Transition: A History of the Latter-day Saints, 1890–1930*, pp. 16–36, by Thomas G. Alexander. (Urbana: University of Illinois Press, 1986)

[18] *World War I and the origin of Civil Liberties in the United States.* Paul L. Murphy, New York 1979

Protestants

The American Protestant views of the war defy simple categorization and analysis. Many denominations spoke in jingoist patriotic phrases calling for immediate punishment and retributions.

Billy Sunday, the most popular patriot-evangelist of his day, saw the war as good against evil, God against Satan.

He also saw a God-given opportunity to confront the anti-Christ teachings of evolution, social Darwinism, higher criticism and every other philosophical evil of the age.

Harry Emerson Fosdick, the most eloquent American Protestant statesmen of his time, supported America's entry into the war but came out of it a confirmed pacifist. Reflecting the utter disillusionment the war wrought on many religionists: "There is nothing glamorous about war any more..."

Francis A. Schaeffer, author of *A Christian Manifesto*, stated,

> "I am not a pacifist because pacifism in this fallen world in which we live means to desert the people who need our greatest help. There was no possible way to stop the awful terror that was occurring in Hitler's Germany except by the use of force. Because of the fall it is not the way God meant it to be."[19]

*****

---

[19] Speech delivered in Washington D.C. in 1982

Hutterites

Hutterites, like other pacifist Christian sects, found themselves conscripted, whether married or not. Of course, they refused to carry a weapon or put on the uniform of their country. The young men had the finest reputation as hard workers more than willing to perform difficult and dangerous civilian service alternatively. To make examples of them, the government of that time refused exemption. The young Hutterite men were abused terribly and mistreated as a matter of course. Thrown into jail cells in Alcatraz Island and Leavenworth, Kansas with the vilest of professional criminals, sadist and perverts; their wives and families despaired for their desperate plight.

In one instance, two of the young married Brothers from the Rockport Colony were brutally tossed into solitary confinement where they died from their mistreatment, martyrs to their church. Although they refused to put on a military uniform, a government-issued uniform was put on their corpses for their burial! An example was made to all.

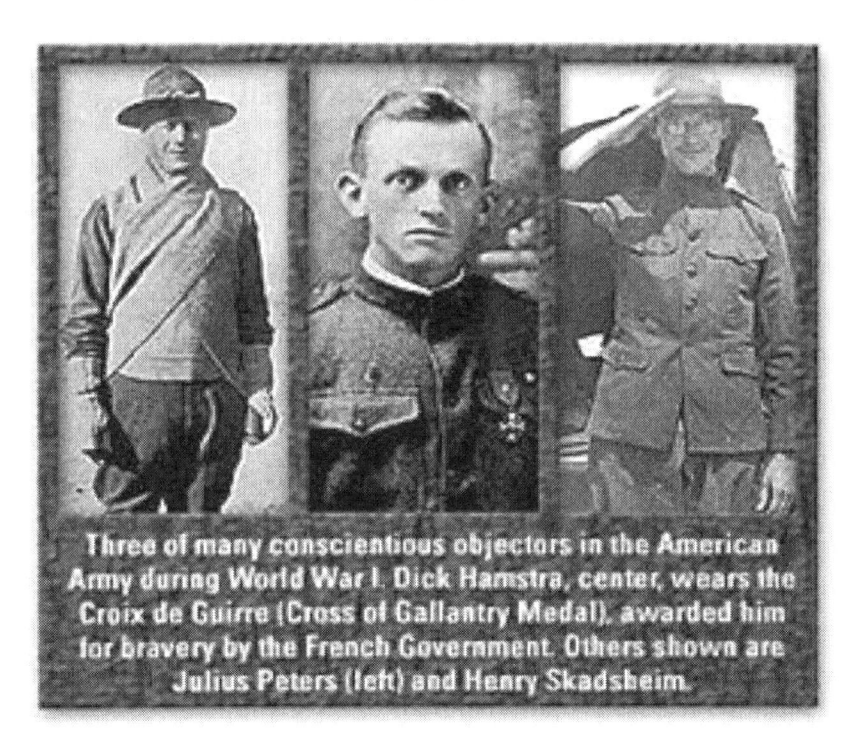

*****

Three of many conscientious objectors in the American Army during World War I. Dick Hamstra, center, wears the Croix de Guirre (Cross of Gallantry Medal), awarded him for bravery by the French Government. Others shown are Julius Peters (left) and Henry Skadsheim.

Seventh-day Adventists

"RESOLVED, it is the judgment of this Conference, the bearing of arms, or engaging in war, is a direct violation of the teachings of our Savior and of the spirit and letter of the law of God." (5th annual conference of the Church of Seventh-day Adventists, 1867.)

Seventh-day Adventists sought a fine balance between civil and God's authority without identifying themselves as outsiders or radical absolutists who posed a threat to the security of others.

If each member could attune his conscience properly, neither disloyalty to their country nor any insult to God would transpire.

The first test of this ideal arrived because of their unanimous opposition to slavery at the advent of the Civil War. A way had to be found to show solidarity with the South without compromising fierce denunciation of slave ownership. The future of the Adventist Church may well have rested upon the solution to this moral tension. One proposal came from Church organizer James White in August of 1862, to wit: Adventists who were drafted into the army should submit to that authority by offloading the moral responsibility to their Government and Generals.

The authoritative solution came from Ellen White, seer and visionary of the Church, who bespoke no courting of martyrdom by rashness of speech while maintaining obedience to officers in the field was incumbent on Christians in concert with Romans 13.1.

A federal draft law commenced in 1863 allowing any man drafted into military service the alternative of paying a hefty fee to commute his citizen's duty. The Adventists community pooled resources and availed themselves of this offset.

In 1864, for a commutation of duty to be purchased by a conscientious objector, it was necessary he be a member of a church officially recognized as such by the government.

The Adventists responded by seeking recognition of their church and by proposing alternate hospital duty for respite. Despite all reasonable efforts on their part, Adventists found themselves molested, imprisoned and refused legal redress. General Conference of 1865:

"While we thus cheerfully render to Caesar the things which the Scriptures show to be his, we are compelled to decline all participation in acts of war and bloodshed as being inconsistent with the duties enjoined upon us by our divine Master toward our enemies and toward all man-kind."

Ellen White, prophetess of the Church, pronounced officially what a fine thing it was that Adventists could perform military exercises because of their subjection to "Superior Authority." This set the notion in place not to resist required service.

Among European Adventists, refusing to carry weapons led to floggings and court martial. In the 1930's on the eve of WWII, Soviet studies revealed Adventists were the third largest religious group refusing military arms.

Church leaders monitored the ebb and flow of patriotic emotionalism and sought to admonish and counsel young upstarts carried away with the sentiments of their fellow citizens by preaching, "We have no business whatever to become aroused and stirred by the spirit [of war] that is abroad in the land." (President George A. Irwin.)

The crisis of sentiment had first been debated among the Adventists in April of 1917 because of a split in feelings about whether a Christian should accept alternate service or remain absolutist.

Affirming their loyalty to their country, their petition declared:

> "...we be required to serve our country only in such capacity as will not violate our conscientious obedience to the law of God as contained in the Decalogue, interpreted in the teachings of Christ and exemplified in His life."

"The wartime Selective Service laws only allowed for noncombatant alternate service and made no allowance for conscientious exemptions.

"Patriotic Adventists wished to reinforce the willing service of duty by "seeking to assist the government in every way possible, aside from the work of actually bearing arms."[20]

****

Each religious denomination produced beliefs and arguments based on the same scriptures and Bible admonitions according to individual conscience.

Was it possible, when at odds with each other's personal convictions, Christians could avoid treating the other as an enemy?

The Christians who fought for their country and their family had little use for other Christians who saw such participation in war as ungodly. Brother against brother and conscience against conscience led to persecution and rough justice. In a war of words, only actions count.

*****

Perhaps the finest example of integrity in the face of persecution in modern times can be found in a most remarkable true-life story which follows.

---

[20] *New York Times*, August 27, 2011, Opinion page.

Medal of Honor for a Conscientious Objector

Corporal Desmond Doss had been the butt of jokes, hatred and ridicule through weeks of basic training, with only his pocket Bible to sustain and comfort him. His wife had presented it to him as a cherished gift on their wedding day. Now, Doss was a volunteer in the army and a medic but he was also a pacifist Seventh-day Adventist. To his combat battalion this only meant one thing; he was too cowardly to fight. Month after month of combat went by at Guam, Leyte and Okinawa and it was always the same. He would be praying and feel some soldier's boot hit him in the back and hear the curses of his own men. Now it was the eve of battle at the foot of the Maeda Escarpment where a Japanese regiment lay in wait in caves and tunnels with hundreds of weapons aimed down that 400 foot cliff pointed straight at Company B, 77th Infantry Division and medic Desmond Doss.

On the eve of battle that April morning in 1945, the orders had come. The division was to scale the 400 foot cliff and swarm the entrenchments and root out all the Japanese skulking there.

The war-hardened Japanese troops would fight to the last man defending the rocky fortress and the odds of taking the escarpment were too huge to even contemplate. Corporal Doss reached into his top pocket and pulled out his Bible and offered to pray for the men. Immediately the sneers began, "Fellows, come over here, gather around. Doss wants to pray for us!"

Jeers and curses were hurled and one of the men said out loud that his intention was to shoot the medic in the back first chance he got in the heat of battle. Doss just shrugged and said, "I believe prayer is the best life saver there is. The men should really pray before going up." Doss was teased, harassed and ridiculed, but he prayed for them anyway.

The major struggle began. The Americans started climbing, shooting and clinging to the cliff sides fighting not only a well-entrenched and often camouflaged enemy, but formidable terrain. Upon reaching the summit, Company B was immediately pinned down by heavy enemy fire. To the left, Company A was fighting to scale their sector as well. The first five men were killed and casualties mounted to the point that Company A could proceed no farther. Headquarters radioed Company B for a report of their own casualties. So far there had been none.

So the order was given that Company B would have to take the escarpment themselves. Sweeping across the cliff face, the men of Doss' company engaged the enemy in a fierce struggle, knocking out eight or nine pillboxes. By day's end they emerged victorious. Not a single man was killed and the only wounds were sustained by one soldier in Company B whose hand was damaged by a falling rock. It was incredible... even miraculous.

The next day an inquiry came up to the officer in command. How had they taken the escarpment without losing a single man? The Sergeant thought about it for a moment and wrote, "Doss prayed."

Three days after the initial assault, Doss had braved a hail of enemy rifle and mortar fire to rush 200 yards forward of the lines to rescue a wounded soldier.

Two days later four soldiers who were assaulting an enemy gun emplacement fell. Doug Sterner tells the story:

"Desmond ignored the rain of enemy grenades around him to rush to their aid. Moving to within 8 yards of the mouth of the cave from which the enemy had cut down his fellow soldiers, Doss made 4 separate trips to reach and rescue the wounded."

"On May 5th the tide of battle turned against the Americans."

"Enemy artillery, mortars and machine gun fire began to rake into the ranks of Company B, 77th Infantry Division. Japanese soldiers swarmed out of their foxholes and caves in every direction. Almost immediately 75 men fell wounded and the remaining men were forced to fall back and retreat to the base of the escarpment. The only soldiers remaining at the top of the cliff were the wounded, the Japanese and Desmond T. Doss."

"Heedless of the shells bursting around him and the bullets directed his way, Desmond tended his injured comrades. At the base of the escarpment those few soldiers who had managed to escape the onslaught could only sit helplessly by and hear the sounds of the battle as the wounded struggled to survive atop the cliff. And then—amazingly—a wounded soldier appeared over the face of the escarpment."

"Dangling from a rope, he slowly descended to the safety of its base as a tall medic fed the rope through his hands from the summit. First one, then another and another and another, heedless of the advancing Japanese, Desmond Doss went about the work of sending the wounded to safety."

"Reports of that day tell of Japanese advancing with rifles and bayonets to within a few feet of the medic, slowly lowering his men to safety, before one of the wounded could kill the enemy before they shot Doss."

"For five hours Doss lowered soldier after soldier down the face of the escarpment, using little more than a tree stump to wind the top edge of the rope around."

"Throughout the five hours, Desmond had only one thought," military historian Doug Sterner continues, "he prayed, 'Lord, help me get one more. Just *one* more!'"

"How many men had Doss saved that day? One hundred and fifty-five soldiers went up the escarpment that day and only 55 were able to retreat without assistance."

"The Army determined the conscious objector had saved 100 lives. 'Couldn't be,' Desmond had replied. 'It couldn't have been more than 50. I wouldn't have had the time to save 100 men.'"

"The bloody struggle for the Maeda Escarpment continued for weeks. On the night of May 21st, the Americans launched a bold attack. When the return fire forced the Americans to take cover, Desmond remained in the open to treat the wounded."

"He and three other soldiers crawled into a hole to wait out the darkness. Suddenly a grenade landed among them. Three men scrambled out, but Desmond was too late. Reflexively he covered the grenade with his boot, and then felt it detonate beneath him and hurl his body into the darkness of night."

"When he fell back to earth the leg was still there, but bleeding badly from numerous wounds. Rather than call for another medic to leave shelter and risk his own life, Desmond bandaged his own wounds and waited the five hours alone until daylight broke."

"As the litter bearers arrived with the dawn and began to carry the wounded medic out of danger they passed another critically wounded soldier."

"Desmond instructed them to put down his litter, then rolled off it and told them to take the other man. While he awaited their return he was joined by yet another wounded soldier. Together the two of them set out for safety, leaning upon each other."

"Once again rifle fire split the morning. Pain stabbed Desmond's arm which was curled across the shoulders of his new comrade. The sniper's bullet went into his wrist, exited through his elbow and then lodged itself in his upper arm. Had the bullet not hit Doss, it probably would have struck his wounded compatriot in the neck. Desmond borrowed his friend's rifle and used the stock to fashion a splint for his useless arm. Then the two continued to crawl to safety."

"Seventeen pieces of shrapnel were removed from Desmond's leg and his arm was set in a sling."

"On the hospital ship Desmond was being prepared for the return home. That's when he discovered he had lost his beloved Bible. It was probably lying next to a puddle of his own blood up on the awful cliff."

"His incredible mission accomplished, a physically exhausted Desmond Doss had cleaned up as much as his simple surroundings would allow."

"Then he went off alone to read, to pray and to thank God for all He had accomplished on that day."

"At home another surprise awaited the young man. His men hadn't forgotten the brave medic or his love for the Word of God. The message about "Doss' Bible" had been delivered."

"Incredibly, the men who once mocked the Godly Seventh-day Adventist who would not compromise had returned to the Maeda Escarpment with a new mission and purpose."

"After soundly defeating the Japanese they fanned out across the rocky terrain and conducted a search until they found and mailed home, Desmond's Bible."

"On October 12, 1945, Desmond Doss was invited to the White House. President Harry S. Truman held a Medal of Honor in his hand as he looked at the brave young medic. "I would rather have this Medal," he said, "than to be the President." Then, with those words, he hung the Medal of Honor around the neck of Corporal Desmond Thomas Doss."[21]

---

[21] *Home of heroes*, C. Douglas Sterner © 1999-2013

Conclusions

The conscience of a pacifist or conscientious objector is as individual and unique as fingerprints. No two are alike. All throughout history each pacifist has had individual reasons, feelings and beliefs which justified a refusal to engage in warfare. Each one knows by listening to the inner, guiding voice how far to go and which lines must not be crossed.

If Augustine was correct in his Just War Theory, Christians were perfectly justified in obeying the appointed and duly authorized Superior Authority and the generals who commanded the armies defending king and country. God would judge the rulers for their wrongs and excuse the compliant Christian soldiers. (Note: this principle was invalidated at Nuremburg after WWII.)

****

As long as Romans 13.1 stood as the bedrock of duty in God's honor, a fallback was afforded to sensitive hearts and minds as an escape valve.

****

In the 19th Century, however, a modern religion would arise in which great violence was done to the premise of Just War Theory, Romans 13.1, obedience to the State and conscience before God.

The result of this summary annulment led to hard times and unnecessary hardship for certain people of faith. It is to the End Times Apocalyptic Community we now turn for what may well be considered a cautionary tale.

C. T. Russell starts a new American pacifist sect

CONFOUNDING GOD AND CAESAR

Charles Taze Russell, like the early Christians before Constantine, was under the spell of apocalyptic obsessions with the result he and those who were like-minded saw little value in practical thinking.

The so-called *Russellites* were utterly convinced Jesus had already returned invisible-to-the-eye in 1874 and was preparing to snatch them into heaven in 1914.

The early Bible Students (forerunners of the later Jehovah's Witnesses) agreed with all major Christian denominations: divine permission for secular authority (Caesar) was a duty imposed in Romans 13.1.

However, a Christian could not serve two masters when conflict arose; he must obey God as ruler *rather than* men. Needless confusion arises if this scripture is set at odds with itself, both for the man of God and for the man appointed *by* God.

Question: If God is speaking *through* a man, then, who must a Christian obey? One or both? How?

On page 266 of Volume I of *Studies in the Scriptures*, C. T. Russell identified the "Higher Powers" of Romans 13.1 as referring to human governments. He also wrote:

> "Obedience to the laws of the land might at some time oblige us to bear arms and in such event it would be our duty to go into the army, if unable in any legal and proper manner to obtain exemption, but it would not be our duty to volunteer.

> "If it came to the point of battling we above all would be obliged to draw the line when commanded to fire and we could not, in harmony with the divine program, fire upon a fellow-creature with the intention of taking his life. If we fired we should be obliged to fire either into the air or into the ground. . .The governor of the State has the right, under the laws, to call for and to conscript, if necessary, soldiers for the defense of the State and of the nation; and if such requisition be enforced upon us we must render our dues and take our share in the trials and difficulties of the service, whatever they may be"[22]

---

[22] *Zion's Watch Tower*, 15 April 1903, p. 120

JOSEPH FRANKLIN RUTHERFORD

President of the Watch Tower Society from 1917-1942

An in depth examination of Pastor Russell's successor is necessary for good reason. The various independent congregations under Pastor Russell had large numbers of Christian pacifists whose families produced young men about to face the First World War. Two major battles were about to commence: internal and external.

> Mr. Rutherford testified that he was born in Morgan County, Mo., forty-nine years ago, and that for fourteen years he was a Judge of the Circuit Court in that State. He said he was admitted to the New York bar in 1910. The witness said that he became acquainted with the doctrines of "Pastor" Russell by reading his books in 1894, and met him personally a short time later. In 1906 he made his consecration to the Lord, and in 1916 he became head of the International Bible Students Association.

The New York Times, June 18, 1918.

"Judge" Rutherford changed almost everything Pastor Russell had stood for in the course of his tenure as President of the Watch Tower Society. Within 15 years, he would create the new name that only a lawyer might invent: Jehovah's *Witnesses*. In the end, he would centralize the once democratic congregations.

By forcing a showdown with secular authority, instead of submitting to it as other Christians had done, he crafted the provocative re-interpretation of "Superior Authority" leading to problems in years to come, which was *later revoked in 1962 without explanation.*

To this day, Jehovah's Witnesses look back on the years immediately following WWI as a prophetic fulfillment of scripture and self-apply all kinds of divine appointment, selection and approval for their leaders, the *governing body*, which would subsequently be referred to as the "Organization." Rutherford <u>was</u> the Organization.

THE CONSCIENTIOUS OBJECTOR AT THE FRONT!

OH, YOU NAUGHTY UNKIND GERMAN —
REALLY, IF YOU DON'T DESIST
I'LL FORGET I'VE GOT A CONSCIENCE,
AND I'LL SMACK YOU ON THE WRIST!

The traditional Christian Church had adopted the unique view of Augustine; the State was ordained by heaven and a Just War Theory applied when the State called for action. The conscientious Christian bore no condemnation under that interpretation. Duty to the State was approved by Almighty God.

Judge Rutherford was determind to destroy the central idea behind **Romans 13.1** by taking it upon himself to revoke Caesar's rightful authority in 1917.

His interpretation was **changed back to the correct historical view in 1962**, but, not before a world of persecution, violence and imprisonments were brought down upon the brethren! After 1962, the need for the change (before or afterward) was never fully explained. The flip-flop was reckoned *New Light* from Jehovah.

Two incredibly disastrous errors of certainty added up to the loss of life, property and credibility for believers: misidentifying who Superior Authority was and wrongly teaching others to forgo subjection to it.

> "Ambitious kings of Europe armed for war, because they desired to grab the territory of the other peoples; and the clergy patted them on the back and said: 'Go to it, you can do no wrong; whatsoever you do is all right.'"[23]

Most pacifist groups sought peaceful solutions between religion and the State by demonstrating a willingness to be of service. Jehovah's Witnesses rejected this avenue with a certain audacious, self-empowered sense of entitlement.

Judge Rutherford's first order of business was arrogating the release of a *certain* book which immediately landed him and the Society's directors in prison! What was behind such self-destruction?

---

[23] 1918 District convention sermon by J.F. Rutherford

Judge Rutherford was creating a Protestant version of the Catholic Pontiff's central moral authority in self-assuming he was *anointed* and it was *prophetic.*

In the Catholic Church, the penalty for insubordination to the official Declarations of the Pope was excommunication as a heretic. Under Judge Rutherford's interpretations of "Truth," he himself was the select mouthpiece of Jehovah (as Russell had been rumored to be). If you disagreed with Rutherford's New Light (changes to historical Christian doctrine) you would be disfellowshipped as an apostate. A strong central control over previously democratically elected congregations assured this governing body an unassailable imprint of primacy.

Russellites, Bible Students and offshoots immediately contested this as a "grab for power."

The Finished Mystery was a compilation of material from Russell's notes and writings plus additional inflammatory materials by Clayton Woodworth and George Fisher. What was in this book that alarmed federal authorities and resulted in arrest and prosecution?

What impact would that, in turn, have on draft resistance?

The eight indicted members; seven imprisoned. (Jehovah's Witnesses: Proclaimers of God's Kingdom)

William E. Van Amburgh (Sec. Treas.), Joseph F. Rutherford (President), A. Hugh Macmillan (Director), Robert J. Martin (Office Manager), Fredrik H. Robison (Editorial Committee Member), Clayton J. Woodworth (Author), George H. Fisher (Author), Giovanni De Cecca (Italian Translation Dept.)

Judge Rutherford began predicting the dead would rise to life on a paradise earth by 1925. Along with that prediction a catchy promise was made: MILLIONS NOW LIVING WILL NEVER DIE. Time has disproved Rutherford and made tatters of his *anointed* veracity.

"Worse than traitors"

Judge Howe's sentence and comments:

> "If they had taken guns and swords and joined the German Army, the harm they could have done would have been insignificant compared with the results of their propaganda."

> "They are worse than traitors. You can catch a traitor and know what he is about. But you cannot catch a man who does what they did under the guise of religion. Do you agree with me, Judge?" Judge Oeland nodded his head in approval."

> The Federal Grand Jury indictment, under which Rutherford and his associates were arrested, charges them with "unlawfully and willfully conspiring to cause insubordination, disloyalty, and refusal of duty of the military and naval forces of the United States."
> There are four counts in the indictment, all charging disloyalty.
> The indictment was based largely upon matter published in the Watch Tower and Kingdom News, publications issued by the society, and "The Finished Mystery," a work by the late "Pastor" Russell. The magazines contain letters written from Italy and having to do with the trial in that country of a member of the International Bible Students' Association for making defamatory remarks about military service.

- *New York Times*, May 9, 1918 -

He said that when criticism was directed toward "The Finished Mystery" he went to Washington and asked the authorities to censor the book, but that they refused. Mr. Rutherford denied that he had ever entered into a conspiracy against the Selective Conscription act, or did anything to obstruct the Government in its preparations for war, but admitted that as a "consecrated Christian" he was opposed to war in any form.

In the indictment against the men the first count charged that they willfully conspired to cause insubordination, disloyalty, and refusal of duty in the military forces of the United States. The second charged that the defendants conspired willfully to obstruct the recruiting and enlistment service of the United States. The third that they willfully attempted to cause insubordination, and the fourth count that they willfully attempted to obstruct the recruiting and enlistment service of the country.

New York Times, June 18, 1918

Rutherford published a coerced appeal promoting War Bonds! He agreed to remove certain offending passages.

Soldiers who were already serving in the military wrote conscientious letters to the Watchtower asking heart-breaking questions and seeking guidance.

Letters to Bible Students in Military Camps

"There is only one of two things you can do—go to war, or refuse to take a part in the conflict in any way and receive the consequences...If you feel you cannot have anything to do with the present war, you will refuse and let the officials take their course. You probably will be confined or shot. Probably the Lord wants some of His saints in prison for a while to tell the element they meet there that the Kingdom of Heaven is at hand and soon all their sufferings will cease . . . If you are shot because of the stand you take for the Lord, that will be a quick method of entering His glorious presence."[24]

"We can serve only one Master. If we obey the earthly captain we must disobey our Heavenly captain. If we obey our Heavenly captain, we must disobey our earthly captain, one of the two, which shall we obey?...If we believe that this war is the last one and that all the kingdom must go down, so the kingdom of Christ be established, should we have any part in the military service?"[25]

---

[24] J.F. Rutherford, WT Society President
[25] John De Cecca, WT Society, Board of Directors

In 1919, the Bible Students obtained 700,000 signatures in a petition directed towards President Woodrow Wilson on behalf of the imprisoned members. After WWI ended and the case was overturned on a Writ of Error without prosecution seeking another trial, the Society claimed exoneration, but this is inaccurate. The trial *errors* meant certain *procedures* must be corrected and retried.

The war was over. Everybody involved wanted to move forward and put the war and its woes behind them. That was that and it was a time for moving forward with hope.

The Government was not out to get Rutherford and the Bible Students. If this had been the case, they could have had a new trial, corrected the errors and still convicted them. The purpose of the anti-sedition laws during wartime had been served and there was no further interest in keeping zealots in jail.

AFTERMATH

Historically, men and women of conscience were peaceful, no matter what religious, moral or ethical motivation stirred them toward their views. As Christians, they remained committed to harmony and agreement by seeking to quell animosity.

Why were Witness leaders driving this antagonism in view of the disastrous consequences? Excessively confident of their own stance, they erred on the side of hubris. No humility or lowliness of mind seemed to be operating in either the words spoken or published.

Jehovah's Witnesses vs. Superior Authorities

The early Christians in the Roman Empire had been mocked and abused as *atheists* because they did not believe in plural deities as the surrounding pagans did.

Early Christians moved in small cells of believers from household to household with private ceremonies, prayers and praise. If challenged publicly to account for themselves they would not shrink from giving testimony, but there is no instance of any agent provocateurs among them inciting retributions against the movement as a whole.

Under the fascist tyrant, Nero, Christians went peaceably to their death rather than renounce their faith in Christ and without resisting in any way.

Jehovah's Witnesses, in their own era of fascist tyrants, created a public nuisance which brought reprisals of a disastrous nature upon them. Why? Hubris among leadership was visiting Nemesis upon them.

First Amendment actions before the Supreme Court

Jehovah's Witnesses followed a strategy concocted by the legal mind of their president. Witnesses were urged to ignore local laws and ordinances and challenge authority.

The legal department of the Watch Tower Society selected cases with the best prospects for battle all the way to the Supreme Court. This proved problematic.

Let us consider one case in particular:

In the first year of World War II, a Jehovah's Witness named Walter Chaplinsky was delivering the same message Watch Tower Society Judge Rutherford so often preached on the radio and in recordings played to householders on a phonograph record. His choice of pulpit was eccentric by common standards: the public sidewalk in downtown Rochester!

Chaplinsky passed out pamphlets, tracts and magazines with the catchy slogan, "Religion is a snare and a racket!" The town folk did not respond too kindly to having their beliefs denigrated publicly.

The town marshal, James Bowering, stopped by and cautioned Chaplinsky to "keep it down and try to avoid a commotion" as was stirring.

Then, the officer left. Chaplinsky ignored the advice and went right back to his inflammatory preachments! This, of course, included such tasty tidbits as declaring all priests and ministers were agents of Satan leading their flocks to eternal punishment!

A crowd of insulted citizens gathered around him to the extent the roads were blocked. An incipient riot was in the making! In no time at all, the over-eager Jehovah's Witness found himself surrounded by men challenging him on the eccentricity of Witness beliefs such as refusing flag salute.

Chaplinsky informed them saluting was idolatrous and an abomination to God. In some reports given at trial, a man with a flagpole in his hand had threatened to impale Chaplinsky if he didn't renege on his insults. At any rate, he found himself pinned against a car. Then a police officer arrived. In the melee, the JW was struck by one of the angry citizens and the officer arrested Chaplinsky while ignoring the man who had struck him.

The town Marshall returned to help. Chaplinsky argued with both officers insisting they should be dispersing the crowd and not arresting him for preaching!

Chaplinsky was one of those fellows who possessed a handsome amount of righteous indignation! Suffice to say, what he said to the Marshall got him arrested and resulted in a legal fight which went all the way to the Supreme Court of the United States!

The result went against the Watch Tower Society's expectations, although a year earlier, Chaplinsky and four other Witnesses lost a court case for parading without a permit.

The Court upheld the arrest as legal and appropriate. The legal case established: "insulting or fighting words were those that by their very utterance inflict injury or tend to incite an immediate breach of the peace and are among the well-defined and narrowly limited classes of speech which the prevention and punishment of which have never been thought to raise any constitutional problem."

That's a long-winded way of saying Jehovah's Witnesses should NOT say, as Chaplinsky allegedly said: "You are a God damned racketeer" and "a damned Fascist and the whole government of Rochester are Fascists or agents of Fascists." (Chaplinksy v. New Hampshire, 1942)

Justice Murphy, who wrote the *Chaplinsky* opinion, was known for his sensitivity to First Amendment freedoms. Murphy authored several other opinions protecting the First Amendment rights of Jehovah's Witnesses. But, he ruled against Chaplinsky.

Chaplinsky has had an enormous impact on First Amendment law.

> "Remarkably, the decision has never been overruled," said free-speech expert Robert O'Neil, who founded the Thomas Jefferson Center for the Protection of Free Expression." It is still very much alive and well."[26]

One man's Freedom of Speech is another man's excuse to disturb the peace and incite ill will among his fellow citizens in the cause of evangelism. Each court victory seemed to embolden yet greater and greater indifference to the backlash of hurt feelings on the part of the other Christians whom they were calling out as dupes of Satan and false religion. Where would this lead?

---

[26] *Judging Jehovah's Witnesses: Religious Persecution and the Dawn of the Rights Revolution*, (University Press of Kansas, 2000)

Public witnessing took many an odd turn

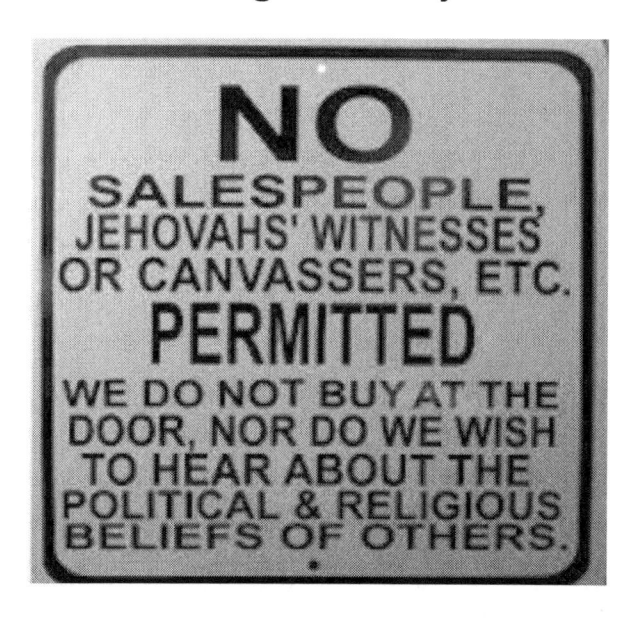

NO SALESPEOPLE, JEHOVAHS' WITNESSES OR CANVASSERS, ETC. PERMITTED
WE DO NOT BUY AT THE DOOR, NOR DO WE WISH TO HEAR ABOUT THE POLITICAL & RELIGIOUS BELIEFS OF OTHERS.

Nazi Era

From the year 1922, the German branch of the Bible Students (called Earnest Bible Students) had been banned for their door-to-door peddling and preaching in the streets.

5,000 arrests were made. By 1932, charges were still pending in 2,300 cases.

Adolf Hitler had laid out his plans and prejudices in *Mein Kampf*, published in 1927. By January 30, 1933, Hitler had assumed enough political leverage as Chancellor to act upon what he had written.

J. F. Rutherford and Nathan Knorr had visited the German Branch Overseer, Paul Balzereit, and drafted a **Declaration of Facts**. Two million copies were distributed to German officials and Chancellor Hitler himself, the Reichskanzler.

"Dear Reichskanzler,

The Brooklyn headquarter of the Watch Tower Society is pro German in an exemplary way and has been so for many years. For that reason, in 1918, the president of the Society and seven members of the board of directors were sentenced to 80 years in prison, because the president refused to use two of the magazines published in America under his direction for war propaganda against Germany. These two magazines, "The Watchtower" and "Bible Student" were the only magazines in America which refused to engage in anti-German propaganda and for that reason were prohibited and suppressed in America during the war.

In the very same manner, in course of the recent months the board of directors of our Society not only refused to engage in propaganda against Germany, but has even taken a position against it. The enclosed Declaration underlines this fact and emphasizes that the people leading in such propaganda (Jewish businessmen and Catholics) also are the most rigorous persecutors of the work of our Society and its board of directors. This and other Statements of the Declaration are meant to repudiate the slanderous accusation, that Bible Researchers are supported by the Jews.

The conference of five thousand delegates also noted - as is expressed in the Declaration - that the Bible Researchers of Germany are fighting for the very same high ethical goals and ideals which also the national government of the German Reich proclaimed respecting the relationship of humans to God, namely: honesty of the created being towards its creator.

The conference came to the conclusion that there are no contradictions when it comes to the relationship between the Bible Researchers of Germany and the national government of the German Reich.

To the contrary, referring to the purely religious and unpolitical goals and efforts of the Bible Researchers, it can be said that these are in full agreement with the identical goals of the national government of the German Reich. We are looking forward to your kind approval, which we hope to receive soon, and want to assure our highest respect to you, honorable Mr. Reichskanzler.

Yours faithfully,

Watch Tower Bible and Tract Society Magdeburg"

Judge Rutherford had formerly proclaimed himself a pro-Zionist "friend of the Hebrew people" much like his predecessor, Pastor C. T. Russell, yet an indecent deep-seated anti-Semitism seemed to boil to the surface on occasion.

For example, while giving a sermon on biblical prophecies concerning the return of the Jews to Palestine at a Canadian Bible Student convention in Winnipeg, Manitoba, in the early 1920s, he blurted:

> "I'm speaking of the Palestine Jew, not the hooked-nosed, stooped-shouldered little individual who stands on the street corner trying to gyp you out of every nickel you've got."[27]

---

[27] *Jehovah's Witnesses, Anti-Semitism and the Third Reich: The Watch Tower Society's Attempted Compromise with Nazism* by Prof. M. James Penton University of Lethbridge

His true opinions of the Jews are reflected in his writings of that era:

> "Be it known once and for all that those profiteering, conscienceless, selfish men who call themselves Jews, and who control the greater portion of the finances of the world and the business of the world, will never be the rulers in this new earth. God would not risk such selfish men with such an important position.[28]
>
> Jews [are] no longer important to God . . .the Balfour Declaration, sponsored by the heathen governments of Satan's organization, came forth, recognized the Jews, and bestowed upon them great favors. The Jews have received more attention at their hands than they really deserved."[29]

On June 25, 1933, seven thousand Jehovah's Witnesses at their Berlin Convention adopted a "Declaration of Facts" to demonstrate they were in full accord with the high ideals of the Nazis. Therefore, Earnest Bible Students should not be banned by Hitler.

Millions of copies of the "Declaration" were distributed throughout Germany.[30] It presented Witnesses in the best possible light *vis-à-vis* the Nazi anti-Jew policies, stating:

---

[28] *The Golden Age* 1927 Feb 23 p. 343
[29] *Vindication - Book II* (1932) pp. 257, 258
[30] *1934 Yearbook of Jehovah's Witnesses*, p. 131

"We are the faithful followers of Christ Jesus and believe upon Him as the Savior of the world, whereas the Jews entirely reject Jesus Christ and emphatically deny that he is the Savior of the world sent of God for man's good. ...

The greatest and the most oppressive empire on earth is the Anglo-American Empire. By that is meant the British Empire, of which the United States of America forms a part. It has been the commercial Jews of the British-American Empire that have built up and carried on Big Business as a means of exploiting and oppressing the peoples of many nations. This fact particularly applies to the cities of London and New York, the stronghold of Big Business.

This fact is so manifest in America that there is a proverb concerning the city of New York which says: The Jews own it, the Irish Catholics rule it, and the Americans pay the bills."[31]

The "Declaration" maligned the Jews by characterization and resorted to popular prejudice. However, Rutherford grossly miscalculated if he thought the "Declaration" would appease Hitler.

Forty years later in the *1974 Year Book of Jehovah's Witnesses*, an effort was made to *walk back* what had been said and done! A blame-shift occurred, accusing the German Branch Overseer, Paul Balzsereit, of "watering down" Rutherford's words and of being "dishonest."[32]

---

[31] *1934 Yearbook of Jehovah's Witnesses*, p. 134
[32] *1974 Yearbook of Jehovah's Witnesses*, page 107

Watch Tower Society leaders were forced into apologizing in the July, 1998 *Awake!*, absolving Balzsereit.[33] Also, the article quotes only parts of the "Declaration" in order to misrepresent the Statements it had made about Jews.

Rutherford continually pressured the German Earnest Bible Students to ignore the bans Hitler was enforcing. The sect was already banned all over Germany. On June 28, the Magdeburg headquarters were again seized and much literature confiscated and publicly burned, mostly Rutherford's own published writings.

Rutherford insisted German Witnesses hold a high profile and engage in banned public preaching campaigns leading to their arrest. *Watchtower* articles practically encouraged martyrdom. In the November 1, 1933 issue, printed a month later in German, Rutherford wrote:

> "Some will say: 'If in the face of so much persecution and opposition we continue to go out amongst the people and publicly tell these truths, then I fear we may be killed.'
>
> That is true; and probably many of the faithful will be killed because they continue to faithfully proclaim the truth which they have learned in the secret place of the Most High."[34]

---

[33] *Awake!* July 8, 1998, page 14
Source: *Jehovah's Witnesses, Anti-Semitism and the Third Reich: The Watch Tower Society's Attempted Compromise with Nazism*, by Professor M. James Penton University of Lethbridge

[34] *Watchtower*, November 1, 1933. p. 328

What "truth" was Rutherford referencing here? Did it not consist of his own published interpretations of End of the World events in the light of Russell's theology?

For what "truth" were they dying? Hubris was leading to Nemesis for every loyal reader of the Watchtower.

On June 24, 1936, State police and the Gestapo formed a special unit to fight the Watchtower movement. Through a number of arrests and infiltration, it succeeded in bringing the movement to a standstill in September 1937.

Nazi prison wardens offered immediate release to any Bible Student who renounced Rutherford's propaganda.[35]

Of the 25,000 Witnesses and Earnest Bible Students in Germany, 13,400 spent at least some time serving prison sentences.

According to Gestapo files, more than half recanted. This was known as "swearing off." German Branch Overseer, Paul Balzsereit, had tried in vain to discourage incautious publicity. For this he was disfellowshipped and scorned. Rutherford's implacable attitude had cost many fine souls their lives for no other reason than his gamble with absolute certainty.

---

[35] *Historical Dictionary of Jehovah's Witnesses*, page 73, by George D. Chryssides

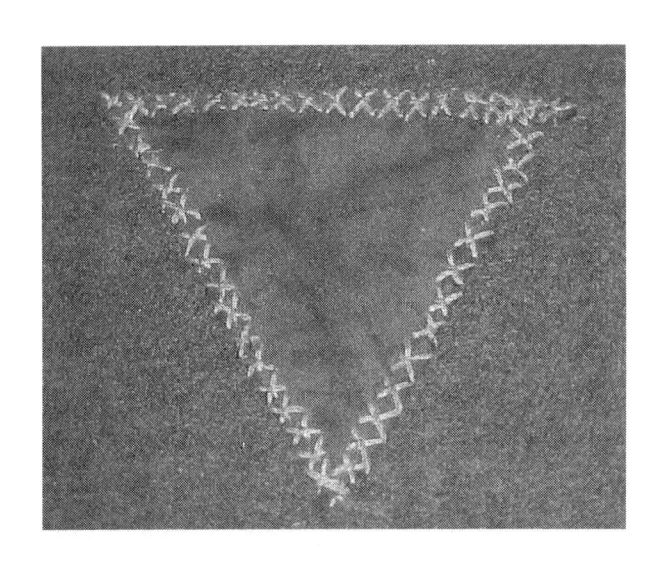

CHUTZPAH

The following action on the part of the Watch Tower Society, in view of its policies and instigations leading to the persecution of its members, is presented here for the sake of illuminating what can only be called *chutzpah.*

The *Holocaust Victim Assets Litigation (Swiss Banks)* CV-96-4849 is a fund to compensate people suffering from the Holocaust. Included is a request dated Mar 3, 2006 to receive a portion of the Holocaust Victim funds on the following basis:

> "Some Witnesses died prematurely and left no heirs to make a claim to the Swiss Bank Settlement Fund.
>
> However, the legacy of spiritual resistance that they left behind is of great value in the education of future generations about the importance of standing up for the dignity and value of human life.

Representing these individuals, the Watch Tower would be pleased to devote any allocated moneys solely to the interests of Holocaust education and the remembrance of the prisoners who bore the purple triangle, according as the court might stipulate."

How much of this was really necessary?

The martyrdom of the JWs during WWII had a profound effect on the movement after the war. First, it gave Jehovah's Witnesses a moral boost in the public eye.

Second, it helped unite the community which had fractured into disunity before WWII.

Visitors to the holocaust museum today are told by the tour guide a full one-third of all Jehovah's Witnesses who were imprisoned in concentration camps died due to the brutal conditions.

They were *not* systematically executed like the Jews and Gypsies were. Instead they were treated the same as the political prisoners. They were worked as slaves, barely fed, etc., but not taken to the gas chambers.[36]

BIASED NEUTRALITY

Watch Tower Society efforts at encouraging Bible Students/Witnesses to flout Germany's strict laws might seem unconscionable to other Christians. These true believers actually believed the world was ending. For many of them, it was. JW's still believed Jehovah was speaking through Rutherford.

He was a de facto *governing body* whose every word was such that no Witness in good standing could dare go against him without suffering the curse of heresy.

Rutherford declared Jehovah's Witnesses were "neutral" and yet his description of the Anglo-American Empire as "the most oppressive empire on earth" exposes a clear bias which is self-repudiating.

Suffice it to say, today's Jehovah's Witness only knows the sanitized version of the Nazi Era mishandling.

13,400 German Witnesses spent time in prisons, often for years. 2,000 died. 270 were executed.

Practically nothing these faithful dead were taught was worth dying for nor is it still taught and believed by Witnesses. The "progressive" truth has wiped it away, replacing it with new things to die for.

---

[36] *History of the Holocaust: A Handbook and Dictionary*, pp. 218, 239, 266, 448, by Abraham J. Edelheit and Hershel Edelheit (Boulder, CO: Westview Press, 1994)

The Nazis treated Witnesses as ideological prisoners, preferring to persuade them to conform to the State rather than exterminate them. After all, other than their strange beliefs, they were ideal citizens of the Reich!

Jehovah's Witnesses did as their leader told them to do without questioning or resisting. What better prospects could there be?[37]

Konrad Franke, later Watch Tower Society branch servant (director or overseer) for Jehovah's Witnesses in Germany, was present at the June 26, 1933 Witness convention in Berlin. In 1976, he gave a series of lectures entitled, "The History of Jehovah's Witnesses in Germany." These lectures were recorded and transcribed. Concerning the convention, Franke gave this testimony:

> "What kind of leaders did we have who brought us [into] such dangers—and the danger of faltering under these circumstances—instead of helping and supporting us, so that we could take a fearless stand [against Nazism]. May all elders who are here among us [listening to this lecture] learn something from these examples, and may they recognize their responsibilities in such matters in the near future."

---

[37] *Historical Dictionary of Jehovah's Witnesses.* Scarecrow Press. By George D. Chryssides

TROUBLE IN AMERICA

"A month ago, an Army court-martial at Monterey, California, sentenced slight, bespectacled Herbert Weatherbee, one of Jehovah's Witnesses, to prison for life. His crime: refusal to obey a superior officer who ordered him to salute the flag. Last week the American Civil Liberties Union publicized Weatherbee's story, adding it to the growing list of persecutions suffered by the anticlerical, religious group which refuses to bow before any 'image' or to fight in any war save Jehovah's.

The Witnesses take their name from the twelfth[38] chapter of the Old Testament Book of Isaiah. Their leader, the late 'Judge' Joseph Rutherford, taught that they 'must be witnesses to Jehovah by declaring His name and His kingdom under Jesus Christ.' They claim half a million followers in the U.S., several million abroad. In peacetime their nonconformity got them deep in trouble with local and State authorities.

---

[38] Isaiah 43:10-12, actually

> The U.S. Supreme Court ruled in 1940 that their children must salute the flag in public schools, in 1942 that they could not distribute literature without peddlers' licenses.
>
> Jehovah's Witnesses regard themselves as ministers, but draft boards often refuse to exempt them from Army service.
>
> This week more than 450 of the group's men of military age are in prison for refusing to heed induction notices."[39]

The self-contradictory attitude of Jehovah's Witnesses toward guns, violence, pacifism and such may be difficult for mainstream Christians to grasp because it is so at odds with consistent historical Christianity. The following items may serve to inform the reader with greater clarity.

> Do the Scriptures approve of a Christian's defending himself against an unlawful assault and using force to repel such assault? Self-defense is the right of every man to ward off an attack and to use such force as to him appears to be necessary to safeguard himself from personal injury or injury to his property.
>
> The same right of self-defense may be exercised by him for the protection of his near relatives or close friends, his brethren.

---

[39] *Time* magazine, April 19, 1943.
(http://content.time.com/time/magazine/article/0,9171,884865,00.html)

Such is the law of the nations or States, but that law does not rest upon traditions, nor upon the conclusions of men alone, but finds complete support in the Word of God."[40]

The dissonance of the above Statement is perplexing on the face of it because War is often self-defense on a larger scale. Nations only agree to self-govern for practical protection.

June 10, 1940, Edwin Bobb was arrested for assault with a deadly weapon with intent to kill. He was a congregation servant for the Kennebunk, Maine congregation of Jehovah's Witnesses.

Bobb issued weapons to other local Witnesses and turned the Kingdom Hall into a firing platform, anticipating trouble from rioters. Then Bobb and fellow Witnesses waited in ambush.

Some men showed up in a car and before it was over two men were wounded, one seriously.

---

[40] *The Watchtower*, September 15, 1939, pp. 279-280

(Ironically the one seriously wounded is said to have had his life saved by administration of a blood transfusion without which Bobb would have faced a charge of murder.)

The only firearms confiscated belonged to the local Witnesses. Police confiscated 5 rifles and 2 shotguns from the Kingdom Hall.

Bobb was later convicted of attempted homicide. Attorneys Hayden Covington and Charles Smith were counsel for Bobb. After his incarceration, Bobb worked at Bethel and on special foreign assignment for the Watchtower from 1948 until 1956.

PROMISE OF ABSOLUTE CERTAINTY

The Watchtower
Announcing Jehovah's Kingdom
May 15, 1984

1914 — The Generation That Will Not Pass Away

1 Clarence Ulrich, 1908-1989
2 Arthur Worsley, 1907-1996
3 George Gangas, 1896-1994
4 John Errichetti, 1912-1997
5 Louise Stemen, 1903-2002
6 Dickran Derderian, 1892-1984
7 Ann Rose, 1910-2000
8 Aquilla Zook, 1898-1993
9 Sophie Yuchniewicz, 1906-2008
10 Dr. Willis Stemen, 1907-1987
11 Bernice (Bun) Henschel, 1909-2001
12 Mary Hannan, 1898-1995
13 Martin Poetzinger, 1904-1988
14 George Hannan, 1899-1992
15 Robert Hatzfeld, 1903-2001
16 Babette Herrlinger, 1894-1995

This illustration intends no disrespect toward the memories (or families) of these unwitting victims — victims of a long line of failed predictions by the Watchtower Bible & Tract Society which showcased them on the cover of the Watchtower magazine to the entire world as tangible proof that the generation alive in 1914 would not die off before Armageddon (the end of the world). 14 were long-time members of their headquarters staff in New York and 2 others served there temporarily. All have since passed away along with the Watchtower Society's failed prediction.

Awake!

Why Awake! Is Published Awake! is for the enlightenment of the entire family. It shows how to cope with today's problems. It reports the news, tells about people in many lands, examines religion and science. But it does more. It probes beneath the surface and points to the real meaning behind current events, yet it always stays politically neutral and does not exalt one race above another. Most important, this magazine builds confidence in the Creator's promise of a peaceful and secure new world <u>before the generation that saw the events of 1914 passes away.</u>

Would you welcome more information? Write Watch Tower at the appropriate address on page 5. Publication of Awake! is part of a worldwide Bible educational work supported by voluntary donations.

Unless otherwise indicated, *New World Translation of the Holy Scriptures—With References* is used.

Awake! (ISSN 0005-237X) is published semimonthly by Watchtower Bible and Tract Society of New York, Inc., 25 Columbia Heights, Brooklyn, NY 11201-2483. Second-class postage paid at Brooklyn, N.Y., and at additional mailing offices. **Postmaster:** Send address changes to Awake!, c/o Watchtower, **Wallkill, NY 12589.**
Vol. 76, No. 20
Printed in U.S.A.

Awake! October 22, 1995

Irony

Jehovah's Witnesses are proud of the 47 Supreme Court cases they won out of the total 138 petitions and appeals they had filed from 1919 through 1988. Great irony abounds in this. The Witnesses demanded freedom of speech so they could stand on street corners and demean the religious beliefs of their neighbors.

The Witnesses insisted on religious tolerance in decrying patriotism and refusing to salute the flag as families who lost sons and fathers in the Wars watched in rage. The Witnesses demanded freedom of conscience while the dissent within their own organization was stifled and free speech was silenced by threats of shunning in disfellowshipping.

The Governing Body of the Watchtower organization will disfellowship any member who voices criticism of its policies on child molestation, blood transfusion refusal, false predictions and the treatment of women. Human rights stop at Kingdom Hall doors.

Ex-members are labeled mentally diseased apostates if they voice their disapproval publicly. Only loyalty to the Organization counts for anything.

> "We must hate in the truest sense, which is to regard with extreme and active aversion, to consider as loathsome, odious, filthy, to detest. Surely any haters of God are not fit to live on his beautiful earth."[41]

---

[41] *The Watchtower*, October 1, 1952, p. 59

"Journalism is printing what someone else does not want printed: everything else is public relations."

George Orwell

THE REST OF THE STORY

I was 31 when I walked out of a Kingdom Hall for the final time. I had been blind-sided by what Catholics call excommunication but Jehovah's Witnesses call disfellowship. I had not attended any religious meetings for half a year while my wife of nine years still went to the Kingdom Hall as she had always done.

I had separated from her and we filed for divorce. We had moved from Texas to California in 1974. This was one year before the truly extraordinary event predicted by the Watch Tower religion. Millions of JW's all over the world were beside themselves with enthusiasm for it. The official name for it was THE END OF SIX THOUSAND YEARS OF HUMAN EXISTENCE.

If that sounds unlikely—well, you feel the way I now feel.

Witnesses had been burned before by false predictions and should have learned their lesson. But, it doesn't work like that. You see, people come and go. The older JW's grow old and die (although they weren't supposed to!) Failures which are disconfirming are ignored and never spoken aloud.

Young folks don't consider skeptically that new warnings of Armageddon might be duds like the older ones from 50 years ago. Newbies are clueless!

Ask any Jehovah's Witness today: "Hey, I hear you guys predicted big things for 1975. What happened?"

Invariably, the JW will never have heard anything at all about that! Those who may have heard "something" will quickly claim, "Aw, that's just something apostates have made up—nothing of the sort happened."

Few J-dubs would actually be old enough, like me, to have lived through the build-up from 1966-75, with all its flamboyant speculation, its excitement and its scuttlebutt, not to mention its rumor-mongering that persisted with encouragement from print.

Our number one priority—above education, healthcare, life savings, career or family—was to tell everybody about 1975 and to get them to sit down for the "Bible study" so they could be saved from destruction. Do or die!

How silly that sounds 38 years *after the fact.*

When I moved my wife and three very small children from Fort Worth to Redondo Beach, California, I was trying to escape from poverty and drudgery. Poverty: because I was working a part-time job at $1.65 an hour. Drudgery: because I was a janitor and telephone solicitor.

Full time door-knocking (pioneering) was far less crucial and far less rewarding than the Witnesses seemed to believe. The fact is, puffed up nonsense is all it amounted to, truth be told.

I had a choice of trying to survive financially on $12 a day with a wife and kids to support or quitting the full-time ministry and moving to greater financial opportunity and using my natural art talent to create beautiful things. This life choice was a no-brainer.

I can truly say this move saved my life, but it eventually ended my marriage. Why do I say this?

I had enough intelligence to know I was miserable and unfulfilled, wasting every opportunity I might have for meaningful self-betterment. I felt I was dying inside from false hope.

The other JW's had a saying that summed up the locked-mind nonsense I just couldn't stand any longer. The saying was spoken at one of the District Assemblies of Jehovah's Witnesses for the purpose of engendering action.

Stay alive 'til '75 was the rallying cry which translates to this horrifying meaning: "Don't do anything commonly necessary for yourself, your wife, your kids or your future because you only have to hang in for nine years."

A Fred Franz chronology was published in 1966 which coyly stated "how fitting it would be" if the "thousand year reign of Christ" occurred in 1975 after billions of men, women and children suffered extinction by means of Jehovah's insuperable, avenging angels.

Why did billions of people deserve such an awful destruction? Okay, I'm going to tell you and I predict you will react with astonishment. I'm not exaggerating.

People who didn't donate for Watch Tower publications, who didn't sit down for a Bible study, who didn't join the Kingdom Hall meetings, who didn't get baptized—these people did NOT deserve to live! Yes, we are talking about maybe 4 or 5 billion human beings.

This was for JW's an exciting—even thrilling—prospect because the Witnesses get all the dead people's "stuff."

Sure, J-dubs will inherit the earth and live on it forever as they grow back to human perfection. Why not smile?

The dead of humanity will rise and a fancy reunion will take place. Does that sound exciting to you or like a macabre and creepy cartoon theology from minds out-of-touch?

I, on the other hand, wanted to establish a career in art and earn enough money to live by the ocean with my family in *the real world* and let the Witnesses believe whatever they chose to believe—without me—because I'd had enough.

However, my wife was born into a family—Johnny's family—and those good folks were hardcore believers. There was no way at all she could ever stop clinging to the "Truth" as published by the Watch Tower Bible and Tract Society. So sad to think how valuable she esteemed it.

To keep peace in the family, I continued to attend meetings an additional three and a half years. All the while, I was making new friends who were *not* Jehovah's Witnesses.

Non-JW's are automatically "worldly." This is a clever pejorative label. Worldly people are de facto *bad associates*.

My "bad" associates were charitable, reverent and deeply committed to God through serving their fellow man.

Horrors!

I was befriended by Christians whom J-dubs would call "goats" even though these *goats* were trying their best to get me and my family settled through caring acts of such magnitude I simply couldn't get my mind around it.

Witnesses are not big on acts of charity; they will not give or help people out if they are NOT *also* J-dubs. No way.

Do Jehovah's Witnesses conduct their ministry because they love their fellow man? Or, is it simply to avoid the risks of losing their lives at Armageddon?

Are their entreaties at the door heartfelt or as disciplined as a regiment in the North Korean army under the thumb of a celestial dictator? So many of them don't even agree internally with the *official* teachings, yet cannot afford the pricking of conscience whispering to them, "Something just isn't right." Theirs is a cold love and a forced smile and a troubled peace of mind.

My needs and my family's needs were met by strangers. I was given a wonderful career by a remarkable artist who befriended me and my wife and my children. His name is Ron Riddick. He and his wife ran an etching studio and he asked me to manage production and become a master inker and learn production and sales for gallery distribution.

From my dear friend, Ron, I learned what I now know is a truly heartfelt love for *strangers* in need.

My life had not begun until I met Ron and worked with him and my new friends, Ron Hudson and Don Magno. They released a flow of creative talent formerly snuffed out by years of fruitless and wasteful manual labor as a janitor. There was more to life than the depressing, never-ending Armageddon death watch, knocking on doors and schlepping humbug theology which was always *changing*.

It sounds sappy to say so, but, finally I *blossomed*.

I am still close friends with all three of those guys—and yet—my former best buddy, Johnny, will have nothing to say to me anymore. He is a Jehovah's Witness version of "Christian," but he is constrained by my status as an ex-JW who speaks out disapprovingly when things need airing.

He has tried *on the sly* to keep in touch out of basic decency but the Society has made clear in no uncertain terms the penalty for this hideous crime of disloyalty. He is now silent.

I am labeled an apostate and I don't *deserve* love, respect, friendliness or even his prayers. "Jehovah" says so. Oh—but—wait! Somebody else tells him this is what Jehovah says. That's not really the same thing, is it?

Nobody knows how many current Jehovah's Witnesses live in a limbo of disbelief *inside* the local Kingdom Hall. The penalty for saying anything or doing anything about it would be the loss of fellow members' conditional love and respect.

Witnesses shun their children, their parents and their friends if they fall out of favor. It is heartbreaking and unnecessary by common standards of decency. It is a hostage situation with a phony tag of divine approval stuck on it. *Heartless!*

I know families of Witnesses who have stealthily faded from attending meetings with such quiet anonymity they managed to escape disfellowshipping and loss of family—just *barely*.

Others filed lawsuits over mistreatment by elders because child-molestation issues were not reported to police due to policy avoiding embarrassing publicity to the religion itself.

There are countless millions of ex-JW apostates in this world right now and no one in the Kingdom Hall cares about their welfare. The former *sheep who strayed* can rot in hell.

Legions of betrayed cast-offs live with the burden of infamy as "evil slaves" of Satan. Name-calling by the righteous, you see. "Love your enemies" makes them laugh aloud.

Doesn't that sound pathetic and cruel to you? It does to me. It is also medieval and small-minded rather than Christian.

The message of the good news Jehovah's Witnesses have carried to your doorstep for over one hundred years is called "food at the proper time" and yet it is spoiled, stale and poisonous because it ruins basic human decency, empathy, charity, productivity and ambition. It denies human rights.

Generations of JW children have been given weak, insufficient education and their basic human potential has been stifled and wasted—but for what?

They still think Armageddon is coming and want to *save you* from it—but only if you will read their publications.

The children of Witnesses are conditioned to suffer ridicule for not participating in their fellow students' joys of everyday life such as birthday parties, Christmas, Easter or even Thanksgiving. The only thing they can contemplate celebrating is their friends' *payback* deaths at Armageddon.

JW kids grow up as oddballs, eccentrics and weirdoes because they had little choice while they were young.

If these marginalized young break away as teens and refuse to play the game any longer, they are cut off from their family and left out in the cold emotionally-not that they were previously nourished and pampered. There are no social programs in the Society for young people to enjoy each other's company. The End is near; why bother?

Natural longing for a mate is stifled as though meaningless in comparison to the "joys" of door-knocking evangelism.

Witnesses are so out of touch with humanity, the high rate of loss is counted merely as a "sign of the end" rather than an indictment of their own pitiless policies toward the youths.

If you are seen as "spiritually sick" you likely get little from your Christian brotherhood but lectures and stern reproofs. To admit to human needs or weakness is to be stigmatized.

Is it any wonder these young Witnesses see no future in this religion and are leaving in droves?

So many countless former members now have lives of their own, distinct and separate from their JW mothers, fathers, grandparents and friends who will have nothing to do with them. The door of human decency slammed shut!

Cast-off sons and daughters cannot reach hearts blown icy cold—but—they can reach out to an alternate service.

A beautiful dawning hope lies in volunteer work. Instead of squandering days and nights on the doomsday countdown to Armageddon, former Witnesses can reach out to the afflicted, the hopeless and the truly needy. What possible better use of time can there be? Hospitals, children's wards, women's shelters and rehabilitation centers are crowded with the hungry loneliness of abandoned and hopeless people. Something so much better than drudgery is charity!

Visit them—not to sell magazines, but to encourage broken hearts to mend! Smile at these desperate strangers so starved for a friend and shower them with the benevolent gift of your time. Give your conscience full freedom to fly. Cheer the down-hearted and grace humanity with warmth and tenderness. This is **true religion**. Hearts will smile!

The End

BIBLIOGRAPHY

Beckford, James A. 1975. *The Trumpet of Prophecy: A Sociological Study of Jehovah's Witnesses.* New York: John Wiley and Sons.

Berger, Peter. 1980. *The Heretical Imperative – Contemporary Possibilities of Religious Affirmation.* New York: Anchor Books

Botting, Heather and Gary. 1984. *The Orwellian World of Jehovah's Witnesses.* Toronto, Buffalo, London: University of Toronto Press.

Cole, Marley. 1955. *Jehovah's Witnesses: The New World Society.* New York: Vantage Press.

Daft, Richard L. 1992. *Organization Theory and Design.* St Paul, MN: West Publishing Company.

Franz, Raymond. 1983. *Crisis of Conscience.* 3rd edition, 1999. Atlanta: Commentary Press.

Gruss, Edmond Charles. 1970. *Apostles of Denial.* Presbyterian and Reformed Publishing.

Harrison, Barbara Grizutti. 1978. *Visions of Glory : A History and a Memory of a Jehovah's Witness.* New York: Simon and Schuster.

Horowitz, David. 1990. *Pastor Charles Taze Russell.* New York: Shengold Publishers, Inc. Second printing.

Illman, Karl Johan and Harviainen, Tapani. 1993. *Judisk Historia* [Jewish History].

Jonsson, Carl Olof. 1983. *The Gentile Times Reconsidered*. Lethbridge and San Diego: Hart Publishers and Good Faith Defenders.

Kohn Stephen 1986. *Jailed for Peace: The History of American Draft Law Violators, 1658-1985* (Contributions in Military Studies).

Macmillan, A. H. 1957. *Faith on the March*. Englewood Cliffs, NJ: Prentice Hall, Inc.

Meeks, Wayne A. 1983. *The First Urban Christians*. New Haven and London: Yale University Press.

Penton, M. James. 1985. *Apocalypse Delayed: The Story of Jehovah's Witnesses*. Toronto, Buffalo and London: University of Toronto Press.

Rogerson, Alan. 1969. *Millions Now Living Will Never Die: A Study of Jehovah's Witnesses*. London: Constable & Co. Ltd.

Smylie, James Hutchinson. 1988. "Adventism" in *The New Encyclopedia Britannica.* Chicago: Encyclopedia Britannica, Inc. Vol. I, page 122.

Stark, Rodney. 1996. *The Rise of Christianity. A Sociologist Reconsiders History*. Princeton, NJ: Princeton University Press.

Wilson, Bryan R. 1990. *The Social Dimension of Sectarianism*. Oxford: Clarendon Press.

Printed in Poland
by Amazon Fulfillment
Poland Sp. z o.o., Wrocław